RAHAB

TRACING THE THREAD
OF REDEMPTION

A Bible study based
on the teaching of

———

NANCY DeMOSS
WOLGEMUTH

© 2020 *Revive Our Hearts*
First printing, 2020

Published by *Revive Our Hearts*
P.O. Box 2000, Niles, MI 49120

ISBN: 978-1-934718-78-0

Printed in the United States of America.

Adapted from the teaching of Nancy DeMoss Wolgemuth by Mindy Kroesche, edited by Hayley Mullins and Erin Davis.

As you work through this study, use this space to doodle, color, and meditate on God's Word and consider how the story of Rahab gives you true hope.

FOR WHATEVER WAS WRITTEN IN FORMER DAYS WAS WRITTEN FOR OUR INSTRUCTION THAT THROUGH endurance & THROUGH THE encouragement OF THE Scriptures WE MIGHT HAVE hope. ROMANS 15:4

Rahab's story
AS FOUND IN JOSHUA 2

[1] And Joshua the son of Nun sent two men secretly from Shittim as spies, saying, "Go, view the land, especially Jericho." And they went and came into the house of a prostitute whose name was Rahab and lodged there. [2] And it was told to the king of Jericho, "Behold, men of Israel have come here tonight to search out the land." [3] Then the king of Jericho sent to Rahab, saying, "Bring out the men who have come to you, who entered your house, for they have come to search out all the land." [4] But the woman had taken the two men and hidden them. And she said, "True, the men came to me, but I did not know where they were from. [5] And when the gate was about to be closed at dark, the men went out. I do not know where the men went. Pursue them quickly, for you will overtake them." [6] But she had brought them up to the roof and hid them with the stalks of flax that she had laid in order on the roof. [7] So the men pursued after them on the way to the Jordan as far as the fords. And the gate was shut as soon as the pursuers had gone out.

[8] Before the men lay down, she came up to them on the roof [9] and said to the men, "I know that the LORD has given you the land, and that the fear of you has fallen upon us, and that all

the inhabitants of the land melt away before you. 10 For we have heard how the LORD dried up the water of the Red Sea before you when you came out of Egypt, and what you did to the two kings of the Amorites who were beyond the Jordan, to Sihon and Og, whom you devoted to destruction. 11 And as soon as we heard it, our hearts melted, and there was no spirit left in any man because of you, for the LORD your God, he is God in the heavens above and on the earth beneath. 12 Now then, please swear to me by the LORD that, as I have dealt kindly with you, you also will deal kindly with my father's house, and give me a sure sign 13 that you will save alive my father and mother, my brothers and sisters, and all who belong to them, and deliver our lives from death." 14 And the men said to her, "Our life for yours even to death! If you do not tell this business of ours, then when the LORD gives us the land we will deal kindly and faithfully with you."

15 Then she let them down by a rope through the window, for her house was built into the city wall, so that she lived in the wall. 16 And she said to them, "Go into the hills, or the pursuers will encounter you, and hide there three days until the pursuers have returned. Then afterward you may go your way." 17 The men said to her, "We will be guiltless with respect to this oath of yours that you have made us swear. 18 Behold, when we come into the land, you shall tie this scarlet cord in the window through which you let us down, and you shall gather into your house your father and mother, your brothers, and all your father's household. 19 Then if anyone goes out of the doors of your house into the street, his blood shall be on his own head, and we shall be guiltless. But if a hand is laid on anyone who is with you in the house, his blood shall be on our head. 20 But if you tell this business of ours, then we shall be guiltless with respect to your oath that you have made us swear." 21 And she said, "According to your words, so be it." Then she sent them away, and they departed. And she tied the scarlet cord in the window.

22 They departed and went into the hills and remained there three days until the pursuers returned, and the pursuers searched all along the way and found nothing. 23 Then the two men returned. They came down from the hills and passed over and came to Joshua the son of Nun, and they told him all that had happened to them. 24 And they said to Joshua, "Truly the LORD has given all the land into our hands. And also, all the inhabitants of the land melt away because of us."

Picture your favorite sweater, the one that makes you feel great every time you wear it. Now imagine that sweater has a stray thread. If you start to pull or tug on it, the whole shirt could be ruined. That single thread is woven through the whole garment.

Open your Bible to the table of contents. If you go down the list of funny-sounding names and count them, you'll see sixty-six different books listed. How do they connect? Deuteronomy has Jewish laws, the Psalms are poetry, the Gospels talk about Jesus' life, and Acts tells us stories of Paul's missionary journeys. What could these possibly have in common?

The Bible is one grand story from beginning to end. The common thread of redemption is woven through every page. What is redemption? That is what this study is all about.

In this study, we'll introduce you to a woman named Rahab. Rahab's life points us to God's redemption.

TIPS FOR USING THIS STUDY

As you use this study, ask yourself:

- What does this passage teach me about the heart, ways, and character of God?
- How does this passage point to Jesus and the gospel?
- Is there an example to follow or avoid? If so, how should I seek to change in response?

Each week of study is divided into five suggested daily lessons, but feel free to work at your own pace. Do what works for you!

You may also find it beneficial to listen to the audio series *Rahab and the Thread of Redemption* at ReviveOurHearts.com/Rahab.

The Holy Spirit helps us understand God's Word. He is a gift and a "Helper" who is able to "teach you all things and bring to your remembrance all that I [Jesus] have said to you" (John 14:26).

Secondary tools that can help you better understand the Word of God (but aren't necessary to complete this study) include:

- An English dictionary to look up the basic meaning of words
- Various translations of the Bible (a good online tool is BibleGateway.com)
- A concordance
- A Bible dictionary
- Commentaries
- A study Bible
- Colored pens or pencils to write in your Bible.

We've included group discussion questions at the end of this book. We'd love you to join the discussion about Rahab with the *Women of the Bible* podcast created to accompany this study Find it at ReviveOurHearts.com.

OUR HOPE FOR YOU

During the next six weeks, may you learn that God is near and ready to rescue you through His Son, Jesus. This is true, no matter what you've done or what happened in your past. He can transform your story.

Each week of our study ends with a **Red Thread Verse** to take into your weekend that talks about the good news of God's redemption. We've placed each of the Red Thread Verses in a special section at the end of each chapter for you to come back to over and over.

Spend time meditating on and memorizing the following verse this week:

HAVE I NOT
COMMANDED YOU?
BE STRONG
& COURAGEOUS.
DO NOT BE
FRIGHTENED,
AND DO NOT BE
DISMAYED,
FOR THE LORD YOUR GOD
is with you
WHEREVER YOU GO.

JOSHUA 1:9

Week 1

Big Idea: GOD IS WRITING THE SCRIPT FOR OUR LIVES.

Did you ever watch a movie and think, *I would have chosen someone different for that part?* Maybe the actor didn't fit your image of what the hero should look like, or you thought the actress was too short for the part. But (unless you're a Hollywood casting agent!), we don't get to choose. Instead we buy our tickets, grab our popcorn, and settle back to watch the characters play out the story, according to the creators' design.

Life imitates art. If we got to choose, history would likely have unfolded differently. Awkward Abraham Lincoln wouldn't have been the ideal choice to be President of the United States. We may not have chosen middle-aged Corrie ten Boom to lead an underground network that helped protect hundreds of Jews in Nazi-occupied Holland. From our limited human perspective, there would have been others who would have been better candidates for these jobs.

We're not casting agents for a movie, and we're not God. He sees all things, knows all things, and is working behind the scenes for our good. He often chooses people we wouldn't to fulfill His redemptive purposes in the world—*including Rahab.* If God hadn't written Rahab into the script of history, we wouldn't know anything about her. Yet she offers us a powerful picture of the redemption Christ offers us.

Day 1: *Be Strong and Courageous*

Read Numbers 13:1–3, 17–19.

The children of Israel spent 400 years as slaves in Egypt. The book of Exodus tells how God delivered them from captivity and the Egyptian army by miraculously parting the Red Sea. You would think that they would trust their Deliverer to lead them safely to the Promised Land. But Scripture records that their faith was weak.

According to Numbers 13:31–33, what did the spies report about the Promised Land?

_____

_____

_____

What do you think they believed about God?

_____

_____

_____

In Numbers 14:6–9, we see Caleb and Joshua's response to the people of Israel. Paraphrase their reply in your own words.

_____

_____

_____

In response, God forbade those who had seen Him part the Red Sea from entering the Promised Land. They spent forty years wandering in the wilderness. As we open to Joshua 1, we find that God's people are finally preparing to enter the Promised Land.

As you read through Scripture, it's helpful to consider the context. You can use the 5 Ws and an H method: considering who, what, when, where, why, and how in what you're reading. Read verses 1-2 and apply this study method using the prompts below.

Who...

- Is speaking?
- Is being talked to?

_____

_____

What...

- Significant event just happened?
- Instructions is God giving to Joshua?

_____

_____

When...

- Is this taking place?

_____

_____

Where...

- Is Joshua when God is giving this message?

_____

_____

Why...

- Is God speaking to Joshua?

_____

_____

How...

- Does God want Joshua to respond?

_____

_____

_____

In Joshua 1:3–5, what promises did God make to Joshua? List your answers in the chart below.

God's Promises to Joshua

REMINDERS OF PAST PROMISES	NEW PROMISES

Read the verses below. Circle repeated words or phrases.

> "Be strong and courageous, for you shall cause this people to inherit the land that I swore to their fathers to give them. Only be strong and very courageous, being careful to do according to all the law that Moses my servant commanded you. Do not turn from it to the right hand or to the left, that you may have good success wherever you go.
>
> "Have I not commanded you? Be strong and courageous. Do not be frightened, and do not be dismayed, for the LORD your God is with you wherever you go." (JOSH. 1:6-7, 9)

The Hebrew word in the Old Testament translated "courage" is often tied to the concept of strength.[1] If someone faces a challenge and loses courage, she's going to feel weak and inadequate. But if a person has courage, she will be strengthened and tackle whatever is before her with confidence.

Imagine you are Joshua, tasked with leading millions of people into a foreign land. What might you be feeling? How would it help you to have reminders that God is with you?

_____

_____

_____

_____

God had called Joshua to a task that was bigger than Joshua could handle in his own strength. There were many battles ahead, and Joshua would need to overcome fierce enemies in the Promised Land. Likely Joshua was prone to discouragement and fear in the face of challenges.

What situation are you facing right now where your natural response is to be frightened or dismayed?

_____

_____

_____

_____

_____

How does Joshua 1:6–9 encourage you?

_____

_____

_____

_____

It's likely that Joshua felt unequipped to cross the Jordan River with twelve tribes of people, take over Canaan, and tackle Jericho. This was a tough assignment! Yet he chose to step out in faith.

Many times, we would not choose the tasks that God assigns to us. But God asks us to trust Him. **He can help us be strong and courageous.**

In what areas of life is God stretching you?

_____

_____

_____

_____

_____

How can you intentionally remind yourself to be strong and courageous this week as you trust in the Lord?

_____

_____

_____

_____

_____

Day 2: *A Pagan Culture; a Patient God*

Read Joshua 2:1.

Rahab is the first person we're introduced to in the Promised Land.

What does Joshua 2:1 tell us about her?

_____

_____

_____

_____

We can find clues about Rahab's background scattered throughout Scripture.

Jericho, where Rahab lived, was an important city in Canaan.

Look up the following passages. Draw a line to what each one tells us about the Canaanite culture. When necessary, draw lines from one Scripture to multiple behaviors.

Exodus 23:23-24

Leviticus 18:3-23

Deuteronomy 18:10-11

homosexuality

incest

child sacrifice

adultery

idol worship

occultism

bestiality

In the verses below, circle the practices of the Canaanites that the Lord specifically told His people *not* to engage in. Underline what God told Abraham He would do to the Canaanites.

> "When you come into the land that the LORD your God is giving you, you shall not learn to follow the abominable practices of those nations. There shall not be found among you anyone who burns his son or his daughter as an offering, anyone who practices divination or tells fortunes or interprets omens, or a sorcerer or a charmer or a medium or a necromancer or one who inquires of the dead, for whoever does these things is an abomination to the LORD. And because of these abominations the LORD your God is driving them out before you. You shall be blameless before the LORD your God, for these nations, which you are about to dispossess, listen to fortune-tellers and to diviners. But as for you, the LORD your God has not allowed you to do this." (DEUT. 18:9-14)

The Canaanites worshiped many gods. They had shrines, temples, and idols across the land of Canaan, and their religious practices included things like ritual prostitution and child sacrifice. Rahab was part of that culture. **Yet God chose to write her into His story.**

Consider the Ninevites that God called the prophet Jonah to preach to. What does Jonah 1:2 and 4:11 reveal about the Ninevite culture?

_____

_____

How are the Ninevites and the Canaanites similar?

_____

_____

_____

How is your own culture similar to these two ancient cultures?

_____

_____

_____

What message did God call Jonah to deliver to the inhabitants of Nineveh (Jonah 3:1–4)?

_____

_____

_____

How did the Ninevites respond (v. 5)?

_____

_____

_____

When God pronounces judgment, repentance, not the judgment itself, is the goal. How can we know? Write out 2 Peter 3:9 below.

_____

_____

_____

Rahab and the Ninevites reveal the pattern of God. Even when an entire culture has gone off the spiritual deep end, even when their wickedness is exceeding, God desires for those who are separated from Him by sin to repent and return to Him.

How does this give you hope?

_____

_____

_____

_____

_____

_____

During the 400 years while the Israelites were in slavery, God was giving the Canaanites an opportunity to repent. He extended grace and mercy to this pagan culture while His people were suffering in Egypt.

How did God show patience toward you before you became a Christian?

_____

_____

_____

_____

_____

Write out a prayer, thanking God for His patience toward you and for the free gift of salvation He provides through His Son. Write the names of loved ones and friends who need to know Jesus, and then pray for them, too.

_____

_____

_____

_____

_____

_____

_____

Jericho

Jericho is located about five miles west of the Jordan River.[2] It is considered the oldest city in the world. Archaeologists discovered remains in its location that date back to 8000 B.C.—long before Abraham.[3]

Located near a mountain pass to the north of the Dead Sea, Jericho was a natural place for the Israelites to enter the Promised Land. It was also at a crossroads of a major trade route to the west and east and an oasis in a hot climate.[4] Its location made it an ideal place for the spies to gather information from travelers who would stop at Jericho and bring news of what was happening in other parts of Canaan.

MEDITERRANEAN *Sea*

JORDAN *River*

CANAAN

Jericho •
Jerusalem •

DEAD *Sea*

TO EGYPT *and Sinai*

MOAB

Day 3: *An Unlikely Character in God's Script*

Read Hebrews 11:31 and James 2:25.

What is Rahab's vocation, according to Joshua 2:1?

_____

_____

_____

Some commentators and ancient scholars say Rahab was just an innkeeper. Was she an innkeeper or a prostitute? Let's dig a little deeper to find out.

The Hebrew word used in Joshua 2:1 is *zonah*,[5] which means a prostitute or promiscuous woman.

Rahab's profession is also listed twice in the New Testament. From today's Scripture readings, what did you learn about Rahab?

_____

_____

_____

_____

The Greek word that's used in these verses is *porne*,[6] which is translated "prostitute" or "harlot" and is related to our modern word "pornography." It is an entirely different word than the Greek word for innkeeper, *pandocheus*.[7] It is possible that Rahab was also an innkeeper. Some scholars say that innkeeper and prostitute were considered synonymous in ancient cities.[8]

Why do you think Rahab's profession was recorded in Scripture?

_____

_____

_____

_____

_____

As we read the Bible, it's important to keep in the forefront of our minds that it is a book about God, *not* a book about us. With that in mind, what do you see about God's character from Joshua 2:1?

_____

_____

_____

_____

_____

From our human standpoint, Rahab was not the type of person we could have chosen to help the spies. **Yet God chose to use her in the script of His story.**

Moses was a murderer.
Gideon was a coward.
David committed adultery.
Peter was hot-tempered.

List some other people in Scripture God used that we might not have chosen.

_____

_____

_____

_____

We might consider all of these people to be inadequate and unsuitable for the job God had planned. Yet over and over throughout Scripture, God chose to use unexpected people to accomplish His purposes.

Write out 1 Corinthians 1:27–29 below.

_____

_____

_____

_____

_____

_____

What does it tell us about the type of people who God chooses to use?

_____

_____

_____

Rahab was a prostitute. Perhaps she willingly chose this profession. Maybe she had been used or abused by someone and then cast aside, and her only way to survive was to sell her body. Either way, God in His grace and mercy looked down from heaven and chose to use *her* in *His* plan for the defeat of Jericho.

What are some sins or suffering that you've experienced that make you feel disqualified to be used by God? List them and pray through Psalm 32, thanking God for His unexpected mercies in your life.

_____

_____

_____

_____

_____

Day 4: *Free from Shame*

Read Psalm 25:2–3 and 34:5.

The Bible doesn't tell us how Rahab felt about her occupation, so let's use our imaginations to place ourselves in her shoes.

If your job was to trade your body for goods and services, what emotions would you likely wrestle with?

_____

_____

_____

_____

_____

Did shame make your list? It's unlikely that Rahab was proud of being a prostitute. Whether a situation, such as poverty, made her feel that selling herself was her only option, or whether she chose it because of the culture that she lived in, it's more likely that Rahab experienced pain and suffering as a result of her prostitution. Sexual sin, whatever the circumstances, almost always leads to feelings of deep shame. It never leads to lasting joy.

Perhaps you identify with this part of Rahab's story. You may have sinned or been sinned against sexually, and this has left you feeling ashamed. Or maybe something else makes you feel this way. It could be:

• A divorce
• The loss of a job
• Bankruptcy
• An abortion
• A prodigal child or an unbelieving husband
• The family environment you grew up in
• A failure you'd like to forget
• Mental illness
• A physical illness or ailment
• Or fill in the blank: _____

Write out your own definition of shame below.

_____

_____

_____

Using the sliding scale below, rate how often you feel shame over a past experience.

NEVER   *SOMETIMES*   *ALWAYS*

1   2   3   4   5   6   7   8   9   10

Is it ever okay for Christ's followers to feel shame? Explain your answer.

_____

_____

There's a difference between feeling shame and feeling guilt over our sin. How would you describe the difference?

_____

_____

_____

_____

Read 2 Corinthians 7:10. What distinctions does Paul draw in this verse between conviction (godly grief) and shame (regret)?

_____

_____

_____

_____

_____

Guilt turns our hearts *toward* God, nudging us to seek forgiveness. Shame on the other hand turns our hearts *away* from God, causing us to hide and attempt to cover our sin.

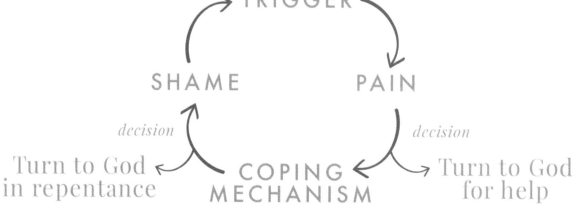

Shame is often a cycle. Something happens in our lives, such as a difficult situation or a reminder of a past situation, that causes us pain. That pain cries out for relief. It moves us to find a way to cope with our situation in some way. It could be shopping or overeating or immoral behavior or lashing out at others or choosing to stuff it down and ignore it—instead of running to God. Then, after we've done this, we feel shame again about how we handled it. Which again causes us pain (because we don't want to sin!), and the cycle continues. Here's the good news: if we belong to Christ, we don't have to be stuck endlessly on this traffic circle of shame. Praise God, there are some exit ramps that can turn us in a different direction.

The first is when the pain comes, **turn to God for help.** Instead of turning on your favorite show for three hours or ranting to someone who can't help you, speak honestly before the Lord. Share your pain, tell Him your emotions, and ask Him to help you. Remember that He is with you in your suffering. He is near to the brokenhearted (Ps. 34:18). He loves you; He will help you.

If you're past that decision point, and you've already turned to your favorite coping mechanism, there is another exit ramp available to you. Instead of wallowing in shame, **turn to God in repentance.** First John 1:9 says, "If we confess our sins, he is faithful and just to forgive us our sins and to cleanse us from all unrighteousness." God also says in Isaiah:

> "I, I am he
> who blots out your transgressions for my own sake,
> and I will not remember your sins. . . .
> I, I am he who comforts you;
> who are you that you are afraid . . .
> and have forgotten the LORD your maker." (4 3 : 2 5 ;   5 1 : 1 2 - 1 3)

God is present with you in your pain, and He loves to rescue His dear children from sin and shame—as He did with Rahab. Turn to Him rather than continuing to live in the cycle of shame.

Contrast Genesis 2:25 with Genesis 3:7–8. What evidence of shame do we see in the lives of Adam and Eve?

_____

_____

_____

_____

_____

_____

What might it have looked like if instead of responding to their sin with shame they had responded in genuine repentance?

_____

_____

How does shame affect your relationship with your family?

_____

_____

_____

With your local church body?

_____

_____

_____

With God?

_____

_____

If you're struggling with shame and need additional help, consider the following resources:

- *Shame Interrupted: How God Lifts the Pain of Worthlessness and Rejection* by Edward T. Welch
- *Unashamed: Healing Our Brokenness and Finding Freedom from Shame* by Heather Davis Nelson

The fruit that God produces in us is joy, not shame. As Christ's followers, we are promised freedom from sin and shame.

Fill in the blanks, using the passages below.

Because of Hebrews 10:22, I know I can _____

_____

Romans 10:11 assures me _____

_____

Philippians 3:13—14 tells me to _____

_____

James 5:16 says we can find freedom from sin and shame by __

_____

If you're struggling with shame and want true freedom, choose to trust that your life is hidden in Christ (Col. 3:3). The sins of your past are fully covered by Christ's sacrifice. You are not defined by your mistakes. **When shame starts to rise up in your heart, hold onto these truths. Choose to believe again that Christ's sacrifice on your behalf is sufficient. Worship rather than wallow in shame.**

Set aside time today to read Psalm 51. This psalm was written by David after he was caught in sexual sin (2 Sam. 11). David turned to the Lord and asked for forgiveness. Praise God in a creative way for setting you free from the bondage of sin and shame. Sing your favorite hymn or worship song, write a poem, draw a picture, meditate on a favorite quote about the freedom Christ gives, etc. Then journal about your experience below.

_____

_____

_____

_____

_____

_____

_____

Day 5: *An Unlikely Character for Grace*

Read Titus 2:11–14.

From our perspective, Rahab was not only an unlikely person to be *used by God*, she was an unlikely candidate for *the grace of God*. We might consider her to be one of the last people on earth to choose faith, but Rahab had heard stories of how God had rescued and provided for His people, *and she believed them.* That's faith!

Think of someone you know that you feel would never be interested in following Christ. How does Rahab's story give you hope for their salvation?

_____

_____

_____

Read Ephesians 2:1–10 below. How do you see the truth of this passage in the story of Rahab? Circle words or phrases that stick out to you. (The text is double-spaced to give you plenty of room to make notes or write down questions as you read.)

And you were dead in the trespasses and sins in which you once walked, following the course of this world, following the prince of the power of the air, the spirit that is now at work in the sons of disobedience—among whom we all once lived in the passions of our flesh, carrying out the desires of the body and the mind, and were by nature children of wrath, like the rest of mankind. But God, being rich in mercy, because of the great love with which he loved us, even when we were dead in our trespasses, made us alive together with Christ—by grace you have been saved—and raised us up with him and seated us with him in the heavenly places in Christ Jesus, so that in the coming ages he might show the immeasurable riches of his grace in kindness toward us in Christ Jesus. For by grace you have been saved through faith. And this is not your own doing; it is the gift of God, not a result of works, so that no one may boast. For we are his workmanship, created in Christ Jesus for good works, which God prepared beforehand, that we should walk in them.

How do you see the truth of this passage playing out in your own life?

_____

_____

_____

_____

No matter if our story is like Rahab's, filled with "obvious" patterns of sin, or if we're deceiving ourselves and think we have no sin, *we're all Rahabs,* unlikely candidates of God's grace.

In Romans 3:9-12, Paul addressed contention among believers regarding who is better off before God, the Jews or the Gentiles (non-Jewish Christ-followers).

He said:

> What then? Are we Jews any better off? No, not at all. For we have already charged that all, both Jews and Greeks, are under sin, as it is written:
>
> > "None is righteous, no, not one;
> > no one understands;
> > no one seeks for God.
> > All have turned aside; together they have become worthless;
> > no one does good,
> > not even one."

Go back through this passage and underline the answers to the following questions:
- Who is righteous?
- Who understands the truth?
- Who seeks for God?
- Who does good?

Look at the passage again, and circle who has turned aside from the things of God and become worthless.

Look up Isaiah 64:6 and write it out below. Underline what our righteous deeds look like compared to God's blinding holiness.

_____

_____

_____

_____

_____

God uses His Word to illuminate our true condition. None of us deserve grace. But because of God's love and mercy, which He showed by sending His Son to die for us, we can be made alive!

Through His Word, God declares that He can:

- Redeem your failures.
- Forgive your sin.
- Restore what is broken.
- Make beautiful things out of our messes.

No matter your story, you are a trophy of God's grace.

To conclude this week's study, look up Psalm 103:1–6, and write out the benefits recorded in these verses of knowing and walking with the Lord.

_____

_____

_____

_____

_____

_____

_____

_____

_____

_____

_____

Red Thread
VERSE

The thread of redemption begins with a story that we would not have written. Adam and Eve, the first man and woman, disobeyed the Lord. Through them, sin came into the world, and everything and every person and society after them was affected. Adam and Eve felt guilt and shame—and realized they were naked. They were unable to redeem themselves. So, they ran and hid from the God that loved them. So, what did God do? Read our Red Thread Verse:

> [Adam] said, "I heard the sound of you in the garden, and I was afraid, because I was naked, and I hid myself." . . . And the LORD God made for Adam and for his wife garments of skins and clothed them. (GEN. 3:10, 21)

God graciously made the first sacrifice to cover them. He hid their nakedness and rescued them from shame. Though this didn't solve the problem of sin, it was the first foreshadowing that a sacrifice that would fully cover us was coming. The story of redemption wasn't over . . . yet.

Spend time meditating on and memorizing the following verse this week:

FOR "EVERYONE WHO CALLS ON THE NAME OF THE *Lord* WILL BE SAVED."

ROMANS 10:13

Week 2

THE MYSTERY OF GOD AT WORK

Big Idea: GOD'S WORK OF SALVATION IS ALWAYS A MYSTERY—WHETHER IT'S IN A CORRUPT CULTURE OR IN OUR OWN HEARTS.

There are a lot of places where we might easily see God's hand at work. The faces of children at vacation Bible school, the celebration of an infertile couple announcing their pregnancy, or the relief of a former patient to hear the words "cancer free." But what about the times when the hand of God is hard to see?

Jennifer Smith was in such a place. Growing up, she often heard from her parents that she was a mistake. Then, she was molested by a Sunday school teacher over a period of four years. As a teenager, Jennifer became involved in a destructive cycle of bitterness, drug addiction, and violence. Jennifer was arrested and sent to prison at the age of twenty-two.

Even though the circumstances of her life were dark, God was working His salvation. Jennifer found a group of people who had an inner joy she couldn't ignore. She heard the gospel and asked God to forgive

her sins. That day, Jennifer was set free from spiritual prison; then ten years later, she was set free from her physical prison, too. Today, God is using Jennifer to share the gospel with women in the same facility where she was once held.

Just like in Jennifer's life, God is at work everywhere—in the dark and hopeless places of the world, wooing the hearts of people in dire situations. That's exactly what He did in the corrupt culture of Jericho as He worked in Rahab's heart. This week we'll explore the mysteries of how God works.

To hear more of Jennifer's story, go to ReviveOurHearts.com/Jennifer.

Day 1: *God Directs Our Steps*

Read Proverbs 16:9.

Before the Israelites prepared to take possession of the land God had given them, Joshua sent two spies to Jericho to gather intelligence on what lay ahead. In order to get there, they needed to cross the Jordan River at flood stage and then enter the fortified city of Jericho. It's hard to know what these men expected to encounter once they arrived.

Read Joshua 1:2–4 below and underline the promise that God gave to Joshua.

> "Arise, go over this Jordan, you and all this people, into the land that I am giving to them, to the people of Israel. Every place that the sole of your foot will tread upon I have given to you, just as I promised to Moses. From the wilderness and this Lebanon as far as the great river, the river Euphrates, all the land of the Hittites to the Great Sea toward the going down of the sun shall be your territory."

Why do you think Joshua chose to send spies into the land that God had already promised to the children of Israel?

_____

_____

_____

_____

_____

_____

_____

It would have been easy for the spies to enter Jericho during the day, as the city gates were open, allowing travelers and merchants to come and go and the spies to blend into the crowd. Once they arrived, God directed their steps to an unlikely place—the house of a prostitute.

What are some reasons why the spies might have chosen to stay at Rahab's home? Circle your answers below.

They had heard about Rahab and wanted to meet her.

It was a good place to gather information and exchange news, since other travelers stopped there.

Her house was built into the city wall, and they could escape quickly if needed.

Rahab probably wouldn't have asked them a lot of questions

Because Rahab was a prostitute, two men going there wouldn't attract much attention.

It was rated #1 on Jericho's version of TripAdvisor.

Joshua told them to go there.

We don't know the answer. We do know that God led the spies to just the right place to find a woman inside Jericho who was sympathetic to their cause and had faith in the one true God.

Share some examples—either from your life or someone else's—of how God directed you to just the right person, place, or thing.

_____

_____

_____

_____

_____

Scripture tells us that God directs our steps and leads us in the way we should go. In the section below, paraphrase what each verse says about God's direction for our lives.

How God Directs Our Steps

PSALM 32:8 _____

_____

PSALM 37:23 _____

_____

PROVERBS 3:5-6 _____

_____

PROVERBS 16:9 _____

_____

As we follow God on the path He has set before us, we'd love for Him to fill us in on all the details. Yet when we surrender our lives to Him, it's more like signing a blank piece of paper, handing it back to Him, and relying on His direction and guidance to show us where to go and what to do.

Re-read Proverbs 16:9, and as a way of symbolizing your commitment to let God direct your steps, grab a blank piece of paper and sign your name to it. Then tuck it in your Bible or another favorite book to remind you that God leads you every step of the way.

We may end up in some unlikely places, but we have nothing to lose in following Him. He is completely trustworthy, and He will accomplish His plans.

Day 2: *God Works through Unexpected Circumstances*

Read Joshua 2:2–7.

It didn't take long for news of the Israelite spies to reach the ears of Jericho's king.

What emotions did Rahab likely feel when the king's men came knocking at her door? She was harboring two enemies of the government in her home. She likely didn't have time to decide what to do. Would she choose to side with her king and her people and turn the two men in? Or would she provide refuge to the Hebrew spies and put her life on the line?

How did Rahab hide the spies?

_____

_____

_____

It's possible that Rahab had done this before—hiding clients from jealous wives who may have come looking for their husbands.

It would have been good hospitality for Rahab to try to protect her guests, but how did Rahab's actions go beyond basic hospitality? What was Rahab risking by hiding the spies?

_____

_____

_____

Read Rahab's response to the king's men in verses 4–5, and summarize it in your own words below.

_____

_____

_____

_____

There's no getting around it—Rahab lied. Even though her lie helped the two spies escape, was it right for her to do so? Some commentators say that what she did was acceptable under the circumstances—that it was not really a _lie,_ but it was a legitimate tactic to throw off the enemy in a war environment.

Then there are others who, without excusing the lie, wonder what any of us would have done in that same situation. What if we had been asked to betray one of God's servants?

_____

_____

_____

Earlier in Israel's history, we find another instance of someone lying in order to protect God's people.

Read Exodus 1:15–21 below. Circle words or phrases that stand out to you. (The text is double-spaced to give you plenty of room to make notes or write down questions as you read.)

The king of Egypt said to the Hebrew midwives, one of whom was named Shiphrah and the other Puah, "When you serve as midwife to the Hebrew women and see them on the birthstool, if it is a son, you shall kill him, but if it is a daughter, she shall live." But the midwives feared God and did not do as the king of Egypt commanded them, but let the male children live. So the king of Egypt called the midwives and said to them, "Why have you done this, and let the male children live?" The midwives said to Pharaoh, "Because the Hebrew women are not like the Egyptian women, for they are vigorous and give birth before the midwife comes to them." So God dealt well with the midwives. And the people multiplied and grew very strong. And because the midwives feared God, he gave them families.

Why did the midwives lie?

_____

_____

_____

_____

What was the result?

_____

_____

_____

Neither the midwives nor Rahab are specifically condemned for their lies; however, nowhere does the Bible condone their behavior either. Instead, the midwives are commended for their disobedience to the king in keeping the babies alive. Rahab is commended for her faith (Heb. 11:31).

Fill in the chart below to compare what God's Word says about lies vs. truth.

WHAT DOES THE BIBLE TEACH ABOUT LYING?	WHAT DOES THE BIBLE TEACH ABOUT TELLING THE TRUTH?
Exodus 20:16	Ephesians 4:25
Proverbs 6:16–19	James 5:12
Proverbs 12:22	1 John 3:18
Colossians 3:9–10	Luke 6:31

God says distinctly in His Word that He hates lies and calls His followers to speak truth instead. Does that mean it's ever wrong to lie if the truth would mean death, as it would have in Rahab's case? Record your thoughts.

_____

_____

Theologians and commentators throughout history have debated this point, with some saying "yes" and some saying "no." Pastor John Piper offers this insight:

> It is possible to be a godly person who walks by faith and yet in extreme situations that are life-threatening, feel constrained to lie in order to obstruct wickedness.[1]

It's also worth noting that Rahab's faith was still new. When God saves us, He mercifully does so despite our sinful patterns. Then, we begin the lifelong journey of sanctification. That's a fancy way of saying becoming more like Christ. Rahab's old patterns, perhaps including patterns of lying and deceit, likely did not die instantly.

Can you think of a pattern of sin God has done a sanctifying work in from your own life? Write about it below.

_____

_____

_____

_____

_____

_____

Ultimately, the point of Rahab's story is not whether or not it is right to lie but that God is at work, using unexpected people in unexpected circumstances to bring Him glory.

To wrap up today's study, reflect back on your own life. Make a list of the circumstances God has used to sanctify you or glorify Himself (or both). As you do, consider how often God uses situations we wouldn't have chosen or expected to bring about true transformation.

_____

_____

_____

_____

_____

_____

Day 3: *An Unexpected Faith*

Read Joshua 2:8–11.

In yesterday's study, we saw that Rahab put her life on the line and risked everything to help the spies. Today, we're going to explore what motivated her to be so courageous.

What reason did Rahab give the spies for why she was helping them?

_____

_____

_____

Rahab specifically mentions two stories of how God had given victory to the Israelites. Write a brief summary of the events described in the following passages.

EXODUS 14:1-30

_____

_____

_____

_____

NUMBERS 21:21-35

_____

_____

_____

Read Joshua 2:9–10 in multiple Bible translations. To make this quick and easy, use an online Bible hub such as BibleGateway.com. List any adjectives or word pictures that describe the way the people of Jericho thought about the Israelites.

_____

_____

_____

_____

Rahab's response to the spies tells us that the Canaanites were living in dread of the Israelites and their God. They were afraid that what had happened to the Israelites' other enemies would also happen to them.

Both Rahab and the Canaanites displayed a type of fear of the Lord. Compare and contrast the two types of fears.

RAHAB'S FEAR	THE CANAANITES' FEAR

Read verse 11. What does Rahab call the God of the Israelites?

_____

_____

In the Old Testament when LORD is written in all caps or small caps in the Old Testament, it signifies the Hebrew word *Yahweh*,[2] the Jewish name for God—the personal covenant name that referred to the God of Israel. This is not a name the Canaanites would have used.

Even though Rahab had grown up in a pagan culture, she chose to place her faith in God because of the stories she had heard. She decided that the God of Israel is the one and only true God, and she was willing to put her life on the line for her beliefs. She knew the strength of Jericho, yet she trusted the God of Israel to triumph over her fortified city.

Read the following verses. The first was spoken by Rahab to the two spies, and the second was spoken by Caleb and Joshua to the people of Israel. Circle all similarities.

> "I know that the LORD has given you the land." (JOSH. 2:9)

> "If the LORD delights in us, he will bring us into this land and give it to us, a land that flows with milk and honey." (NUM. 14:8)

Use the chart below to compare the faith of the Israelites (Num. 14), the hearers of the original message, and that of Rahab.

	RAHAB	THE ISRAELITES
Knowledge of God		
Believers in God		
Strength of their faith		

Do you see the irony? The children of Israel doubted God's sovereign strength (except for Caleb and Joshua), although they'd seen God at work with their own eyes. Here in Jericho, a pagan city, was a woman, who based on her understanding of God from a few stories, chose to place her faith in Him. The difference was that Rahab acted on what she believed (see James 2:25). Her faith was living, not dead. "As the body apart from the spirit is dead, so also faith apart from works is dead" (James 2:26).

What is Flax?

Flax is a plant with yellowish stems and bright blue flowers that's used to make yarn and linen cloth. It was cultivated by the Egyptians before the Exodus.

The production of linen was a common household chore in biblical times. In the description of the virtuous woman in Proverbs 31, she's pictured as someone who "seeks wool and flax, and works with willing hands" (v. 13).[3]

The process of making linen was labor-intensive. First, you had to separate the flax fibers from the seeds. Then, you needed to arrange the flax into bunches, soak it until the fibers were loosened, lay it in the sun to dry, and then re-immerse it in water so it could be bleached and softened.[4]

To dry flax, people would often stack it on their rooftops to lie in the sun, as we see in Rahab's example (Josh. 2:6). After it was dry, they would use a hackle (a comb or board with long teeth) to separate the outer fibers from the inner core. In order to make the fibers into a thread for weaving, the flax would need to be combed again, then cleaned and arranged. Any remaining short, tangled fibers would be used to make a coarse fabric or twine. Flax was also used in torches and lamp wicks.[5]

Has there ever been a time in your life when you've taken a risk based on your faith in the Lord?

_____

_____

_____

Do you need the Lord to strengthen your faith so that you are willing to obey Him, no matter what He calls you to do? Write out a prayer asking for stronger faith below.

_____

_____

_____

_____

_____

_____

In the same way as the Israelites, we can easily substitute the *idea* of having faith for actually living by faith. Some examples:

- We grow up in church, but what we've heard our whole lives doesn't change us.
- We hear sermons on loving others, but we ignore or slander people that we don't like.
- We say that Christians should help those in need, but we don't share what we have.

(Read the book of James for more examples.) Just as God intervened in Rahab's life, we also need God to intervene in our lives and help us *live* the faith we claim to have. Take a moment to consider what faith looks like (or doesn't look like) in your life, and ask God to help you have an active and obedient faith in Him.

The parting of the Red Sea had taken place forty years earlier. Perhaps Rahab heard about it at the time. She believed that the stories she heard were true and that He was the one true God. She was willing to risk everything for that faith.

Think of a younger (or younger in the faith) believer whose faith you admire. End this day's study by writing them a note of encouragement, telling them what you appreciate about how God is working in their life.

Day 4: *The Power of God Stories*

Read Romans 10:13–17.

When God directed the spies to Rahab's home, perhaps they were surprised to hear Rahab's testimony. Her story shows what happens when people hear of God's mighty deeds.

Can you think of any stories you heard about God before coming to faith? Even if you came to Christ as a very young child, you likely heard Bible stories in your Sunday school classes or stories of God at work from your parents. How did those stories impact you?

_____

_____

_____

_____

_____

_____

_____

_____

Whenever the lost world sees evidence of the supernatural hand of God moving in and among His people, they take notice. Some people will be terrified; some will harden their hearts; some will believe. God stories uniquely penetrate our hearts and minds. God works the mystery of salvation in people's lives, but there's a part He wants us to play.

When you were small, and your mom or dad invited you to help with a household task or project, didn't your heart swell with excitement? Isn't this invitation to join in God's work even better?

Read the passages below and underline the phrases that describe God's desire for all people.

> This is good, and it is pleasing in the sight of God our Savior, who desires all people to be saved and to come to the knowledge of the truth. (1 TIM. 2:3-4)

> Do not overlook this one fact, beloved, that with the Lord one day is as a thousand years, and a thousand years as one day. The Lord is not slow to fulfill his promise as some count slowness, but is patient toward you, not wishing that any should perish, but that all should reach repentance. (2 PETER 3:8-9)

Revist Romans 10:14–17. Working backward from verse 15, what four steps are listed that lead to people calling upon the name of the Lord?

-
-
-
-

Before someone can ever have faith in Christ, they first need to hear about Him. God wants us to be the ones to tell them! The Greek word for preacher in verse 14 is *kerusso*, which can be translated as "to publish, proclaim openly: something which has been done." [6]

Even if our job title isn't "preacher," we are to proclaim the gospel and tell stories of what God has done. He sends us not just to far away countries but to our next-door neighbor's house, to the other parents on the school playground, and to that person who sits beside us at work.

Write the names of at least two people in your circle of influence that you could share your God stories with.

1 .

2 .

Take some time to pause and pray that God would provide opportunities for you to share with these people and that He would prepare their hearts to hear. To learn more about how to share your God stories, stay tuned for tomorrow's study.

Day 5: *Always Be Ready*

Read Matthew 28:18–20.

Does sharing your faith feel scary to you? You're not alone.

One Barna research study revealed that, "Spiritual conversations are exceedingly rare for most Americans, and even for Christians, who are at best reluctant to have them."

The study found that 29 percent of Christians say evangelism is the local church's responsibility, while 47 percent of Christians surveyed admit they would avoid a spiritual conversation if they knew their non-Christian friend would reject them.[7]

Is it possible our paralysis is because we're making things too complicated?

Tell your God story! Sharing what God has done in your own life is a way to bring Him glory and draw others toward Him.

Make a list of at least three stories you can share with others about how Jesus is working in your life, your family, your church, your community, etc. No need to give all the details, just jot down a few thoughts as they come to mind.

1 .

2 .

3 .

Record the apostle Peter's words found in 1 Peter 3:15.

_____

_____

_____

_____

_____

Flip to 1 Peter 1:1. To whom did Peter write these words?

_____

_____

Peter was writing to Christians living in territories under Roman control. The broader theme of this letter is faithful endurance of persecution and suffering (1:6–7, 2:18–20, 3: 13–17, 4:1–4, 12–19, 5:9). Living in a pagan culture and under an oppressive government may have motivated Peter's audience to hide their faith. Peter gives them a strategy for how to boldly share it instead.

Specifically, what does Peter ask his Christian audience to always be ready to share?

_____

_____

_____

Notice what Peter does not ask them to be ready to do:

- He *doesn't* ask them to be prepared to recite large chunks of Scripture.
- He *doesn't* ask them to be willing to give absolute proof for the resurrection or deity of Christ.
- He *doesn't* ask them to give convincing arguments to their persecutors about why they should convert.

He simply asks them to always be ready to share the reason why they have hope. In other words, *he asked them to be prepared to share their God story.*

Hope is hard to argue with. No one can debate your experience with God. And if Christ has given you hope, why wouldn't you want to share that with those who do not yet know Him?

Look up Proverbs 1:7. What does this verse say is the path to wisdom?

_____

_____

_____

_____

Also look up Proverbs 29:25. What does this verse warn against?

_____

_____

_____

_____

Perhaps the reason we don't share our faith is because we are afraid of the wrong person. Consider: Has fear of man ever kept you from sharing your faith with someone?

_____

_____

_____

_____

_____

Revelation 12 records a powerful scene. After a great war in heaven, Satan is cast out of heaven to earth (v. 9), and a loud voice from heaven declares, "Now the salvation and the power and the kingdom of our God and the authority of his Christ have come, for the accuser of our brothers has been thrown down, who accuses them day and night before our God" (v. 10).

According to verse 11, the children of God overcame Satan using two weapons. Look up the verse and record what these weapons are:

1 .

2 .

Ultimately, the power to win souls and impact lives flows from Christ's sacrifice on the cross, but we can be a part of it when we share our testimonies, or God stories, with others.

When was the last time you had a conversation with a non-Christian about the hope you have in Christ?

_____

_____

_____

_____

What most often prevents you from doing so?

_____

_____

_____

_____

If a neighbor, friend, or coworker asked you to explain why you have hope, are you ready to give an answer? Explain.

_____

_____

_____

_____

_____

_____

Take time now to answer the question, "Why do I have hope?" As you do, continue to pray that God would provide opportunities for you to share your God stories with those who most need to hear them. Who knows? There may be a "Rahab" in your world who will be drawn to faith by hearing the stories of how God has worked in your life.

Red Thread
VERSE

Weaving its way down from Adam and Eve's clothing, the red thread of redemption continues on to a man named Abraham. God called him to be the father of His chosen people. The only problem: Abraham was old and his wife was unable to conceive children. How would God fulfill His promise? It was a mystery. Until Isaac showed up—Abraham and Sarah's miracle baby. All was going well, until God asked Abraham to do the unthinkable. "Take your only son Isaac and offer him as a sacrifice to me." Abraham obeyed, taking a big risk, because He trusted God would keep his promise. And the Lord did in an unexpected way, as captured in this week's Red Thread Verse:

> Abraham lifted up his eyes and looked, and behold, behind him was a ram, caught in a thicket by his horns. And Abraham went and took the ram and offered it up as a burnt offering instead of his son. So Abraham called the name of that place, "The LORD will provide"; as it is said to this day, "On the mount of the LORD it shall be provided." (GEN. 22:13-14)

Isaac lived, and his descendants became that promised nation. God saw Abraham's faith and counted it to him as righteousness. But what about sin? It was still a problem in the world. There was another promised son coming, who would provide God's redemption—on a mountain! But when? The thread and time will tell.

Spend time meditating on and memorizing the following verse this week:

THE steadfast LOVE OF THE Lord NEVER CEASES, his mercies NEVER COME to an END.

LAMENTATIONS 3:22

Week 3

THE LOVINGKINDNESS OF GOD

Big Idea: WE CAN HAVE COURAGE BECAUSE THE LORD IS ALWAYS KIND.

At the True Woman '12 Conference in Indianapolis, Susan went out one evening for a quick bite of pizza—and got an opportunity to step out in courage.

As she was eating, Susan heard a young woman nearby arguing with her boyfriend on the phone. "You got me into this mess; you're going to have to get me out!" the woman yelled. "You'd better bring me to my abortion!"

Susan felt a strong pull to talk to this woman but had reservations. How would this woman react to a stranger approaching her? Would she think Susan (and all Christians) were nuts?

But Susan couldn't shake the sense God wanted her to get involved. She let the woman know she had overheard everything. Over the next several minutes, Susan empathized with this woman's situation and talked about options besides abortion. Then Susan shared something she didn't normally tell others—the story of her own rape and abortion years before and the regret she'd felt ever since. Moved by Susan's story, the young woman agreed to visit a crisis pregnancy center for help.

When Susan stepped into the situation, she was taking a risk. Trying to talk a stranger out of abortion is taboo according to today's culture. By sharing her own story, Susan opened herself up for rejection. Yet because God values human life, Susan knew He wanted her to speak up, no matter the risks.

When we rely upon the Lord and remember His love, grace, and mercy, we find the courage to face challenges. Through our study this week, we'll see how Rahab's faith in God helped her take big risks to save the two Hebrew spies.

Day 1: *Courage to Go against the Flow*

Read Joshua 2:8–14.

Last week, we saw what happens when we declare the works of the Lord. Not only did the stories of God impact Rahab's life, it impacted an entire culture! Even though Rahab believed these stories were true and that God was the true God, what she did took tremendous courage.

What was Rahab risking with her actions?

_____

_____

_____

_____

Why did Rahab choose to be courageous? (Hint: see verse 11.)

_____

_____

_____

_____

Reflect back on your own decision to follow Christ. Make a list of what you've learned since then about who God is.

_____

_____

_____

_____

_____

In taking this stand, Rahab was risking her life. She was renouncing the belief system of the world around her and saying, "I'm going to stand with the God of Israel."

There are times when we have to be willing to take risks to do what is right, as Rahab did, in response to God's sovereignty. He will give us the courage to make these difficult choices for the sake of Christ and His kingdom.

How did the following people from Scripture risk something to do what was right before the Lord? Draw a line between their names and their actions.

Noah (Gen. 6)   violated the king's order by praying to
                                                 the Lord

Esther (Est. 5:2)   lived in the wilderness and denounced the
                                                 religious leaders of his day

Daniel (Dan. 6:10-11)   refused to bow down and worship a
                                                 golden idol

Shadrach, Meshach & Abednego (Dan. 3)   built an ark to save his family and two of
                                                 each animal on earth

John the Baptist (Matt. 3:1-6)   risked death by visiting the king in order
                                                 to save her people

What other people in Scripture or history risked their reputation or safety in order to follow the Lord?

_____

_____

_____

How do their examples inspire you?

_____

_____

_____

Read Hebrews 11:32–38 and list what people risked for the sake of their faith.

_____

_____

_____

Now read verses 13–16 and consider: Why did these faithful people risk everything?

_____

_____

_____

_____

_____

How does knowing that you have a heavenly city (a home with God) waiting for you inspire you to take a risk of obedience? Are there any areas that fear of man or fear of consequences is causing you to play it safe in following Christ?

_____

_____

_____

_____

Day 2: *A High View of God*

Read Isaiah 6:1–6.

As we saw in Day 1, Rahab had courage to take risks because of her faith in God. Even though she could have lost everything, she was willing to hide the spies because the Lord gave her courage.

Based on what we've learned so far in this study, how do you think Rahab viewed God?

_____

_____

_____

What you believe about God determines everything in your Christian life.

• Your view of God determines if you're willing to go to war against your sin.
• Your view of God determines whether you will be willing to obey God's law even when it's not popular.
• Your view of God will determine if you face challenges with hope and peace or fear and anxiety.

What else does our view of God impact? Make a list below.

_____

_____

_____

_____

A high view of God is based on knowing and trusting His character. In contrast, a low view of God is the result of either not knowing who God claims to be in His Word or on some level not believing He is who He claims to be.

Use the sliding scale below to prayerfully consider if you have a low or high view of God in each area. This activity is designed to help you think through areas that you may be struggling to see God rightly, not to cause shame. Pray that God would help you to see rightly and respond righteously.

How I View God's . . .

I struggle to believe this is true of God = 1
I know this is true of God, but sometimes forget = 5
I fully trust this is true and live from a place of faith = 10

Sovereign control

1   2   3   4   5   6   7   8   9   1 0

Trustworthiness

1   2   3   4   5   6   7   8   9   1 0

Love

1   2   3   4   5   6   7   8   9   1 0

Forgiveness

1   2   3   4   5   6   7   8   9   1 0

Power

1   2   3   4   5   6   7   8   9   1 0

Patience

1   2   3   4   5   6   7   8   9   1 0

Holiness

1   2   3   4   5   6   7   8   9   1 0

Goodness

1   2   3   4   5   6   7   8   9   1 0

Did you discover any areas where your head knowledge about God is disconnected with your heart?

_____

_____

_____

_____

What situations right now are revealing your doubt about any of these characteristics of God? Speak it out loud to the Lord.

_____

_____

_____

_____

On what did Rahab base her view of the Hebrew God? What did she conclude about His character?

_____

_____

_____

We all have a high view of ourselves. It's called pride. What matters most to us in our flesh is *our* feelings, *our* thoughts, *our* ambitions, *our* plans, *our* ideas, and *our* opinions rather than what God thinks and what matters to Him. The Holy Spirit is the only One who can change us and rescue us from the trap of pride.

Throughout the Bible, we find people who had their whole view of God changed after an encounter with Him. Job and Isaiah were two such people.

Look up the following passages and describe how each of these men came to a new understanding of God.

JOB (JOB 42:1-6)

ISAIAH (ISA. 6:1-6)

Although both Job and Isaiah had faith in God, we might say they had a low view of Him until they were confronted with His holiness and sovereignty.

When we surrender to the holy Lord who is the supreme Ruler of heaven and earth—who also daily showers us with His lovingkindness—we will discover joy, peace, and contentment.

Like Isaiah, who witnessed God in the throne room, John had a vision of the throne room of heaven, recorded in Revelation 4. Read the chapter below and circle all the people and beings who are worshiping God. Underline all words used to describe God, and draw a box around how the elders responded to God's majesty.

> After this I looked, and behold, a door standing open in heaven! And the first voice, which I had heard speaking to me like a trumpet, said, "Come up here, and I will show you what must take place after this." At once I was in the Spirit, and behold, a throne stood in heaven, with one seated on the throne. And he who sat there had the appearance of jasper and carnelian, and around the throne was a rainbow that had the appearance of an

emerald. Around the throne were twenty-four thrones, and seated on the thrones were twenty-four elders, clothed in white garments, with golden crowns on their heads. From the throne came flashes of lightning, and rumblings and peals of thunder, and before the throne were burning seven torches of fire, which are the seven spirits of God, and before the throne there was as it were a sea of glass, like crystal.

And around the throne, on each side of the throne, are four living creatures, full of eyes in front and behind: the first living creature like a lion, the second living creature like an ox, the third living creature with the face of a man, and the fourth living creature like an eagle in flight. And the four living creatures, each of them with six wings, are full of eyes all around and within, and day and night they never cease to say,

> "Holy, holy, holy, is the Lord God Almighty,
>> who was and is and is to come!"

And whenever the living creatures give glory and honor and thanks to him who is seated on the throne, who lives forever and ever, the twenty-four elders fall down before him who is seated on the throne and worship him who lives forever and ever. They cast their crowns before the throne, saying,

> "Worthy are you, our Lord and God,
>> to receive glory and honor and power,
> for you created all things,
>> and by your will they existed and were created."

What does it mean for us to cast our crowns before the Lord in response to who He is?

_____

_____

_____

_____

_____

_____

_____

Day 3: *Our Deliverer*

Re-read Joshua 2:12–13.

Rahab knew that God is sovereign. She knew that God had given the land to the Israelites. In addition, what did Rahab know would happen to the people of Jericho?

_____

_____

_____

She wanted to be saved. (As we all would!) Yet in this, we see a foreshadowing of the gospel.

Rahab had violated the holiness of God, and her sin deserved a punishment of death. Since we're all sinners, we deserve the same punishment.

Perhaps by emphasizing Rahab's sin again and again God is reminding us: she was a sinner who deserved His judgment, but He delivered her from her punishment. God demonstrates His grace and mercy in Rahab's life. This points us to the hope of the gospel.

We are all born as sinners under the judgment of God. If God was willing to save this woman and redeem her life from destruction, surely He is willing to save us.

Even as we continue to battle sin as Christians, sometimes God does a mighty work in one moment. Can you think of a time when you were aware of the weight of your sin in a fresh way and you expressed a desire to be saved from God's judgment? Write about it below.

_____

_____

_____

_____

_____

_____

Rahab is an example of God's incredible grace and how He offers deliverance and rescue from sin for each and every one of us.

The Romans Road is a series of verses that are often used to present the plan of salvation through Jesus Christ. As you look at some of these verses below, list how they were evident in Rahab's story and yours.

ROMANS 1:20-21

RAHAB:

ME:

ROMANS 3:10

RAHAB:

ME:

ROMANS 3:23

RAHAB:

ME:

ROMANS 5:8

RAHAB:

ME:

ROMANS 6:23

RAHAB:

ME:

ROMANS 10:9-10

RAHAB:

ME:

Day 4: *The Lord's* Hesed

Read Isaiah 6:1–6.

Write out Rahab's request to the spies in your own words.

_____

_____

_____

_____

List four ways that Rahab dealt kindly with the spies.

1 .

2 .

3 .

4 .

What did she request in return?

_____

_____

_____

_____

Although we know how the story turned out, Rahab didn't. She begged the spies to spare her from the wrath to come, but her life could never be the same. How would Rahab's life change after the fall of Jericho?

_____

_____

_____

_____

Rahab escaped with her life and little else. Yet she seemed to understand her only hope was to cast her lot in with the God of Israel and His people.

Look at Joshua 2:12–14, and circle any forms of the word *kind* that you find.

> Please swear to me by the LORD that, as I have dealt kindly with you, you also
> will deal kindly with my father's house, and give me a sure sign that you will
> save alive my father and mother, my brothers and sisters, and all who belong
> to them, and deliver our lives from death." And the men said to her, "Our life
> for yours even to death! If you do not tell this business of ours, then when the
> Lord gives us the land we will deal kindly and faithfully with you."

That word "kindness" or "kindly" used in this passage is related to the Hebrew word *hesed*.[1] When used of God, *hesed* speaks of His loyal, unfailing love for His people. It's a love that moves God to pursue us relentlessly and persistently. It's His faithfulness to keep His promises to His people that He loves. Even though we may prove unfaithful to Him, His love never ends. His *hesed* is everlasting.

Look at the following verses below, and underline the references to the Lord's hesed (love or kindness).

> The LORD passed before him and proclaimed, "The LORD, the LORD, a God
> merciful and gracious, slow to anger, and abounding in steadfast love and
> faithfulness, keeping steadfast love for thousands, forgiving iniquity and
> transgression and sin." (Ex. 34:6–7)

> And Naomi said to her daughter-in-law, "May he be blessed by the LORD, whose
> kindness has not forsaken the living or the dead!" (Ruth 2:20)

> Surely goodness and mercy shall follow me
>   all the days of my life,
> and I shall dwell in the house of the LORD
>   forever. (Ps. 23:6)

> Your steadfast love, O LORD, extends to the heavens,
>   your faithfulness to the clouds. . . .
> How precious is your steadfast love, O God!
>   The children of mankind take refuge in the shadow of your wings. . . .

Oh, continue your steadfast love to those who know you,
  and your righteousness to the upright of heart! (Ps. 36:5, 7, 10)

The steadfast love of the LORD never ceases;
  his mercies never come to an end. (Lam. 3:22)

I will recount the steadfast love of the LORD,
  the praises of the LORD,
according to all that the LORD has granted us,
  and the great goodness to the house of Israel
that he has granted them according to his compassion,
  according to the abundance of his steadfast love. (Isa. 63:7)

Based on these verses, write out your own definition of *hesed*.

_____

_____

_____

_____

_____

_____

_____

_____

Hesed is also used in Scripture to describe something that happens between two people. It implies loving our neighbors, not just with a feeling but through practical actions by serving them.[2] In Rahab's case, she appealed to the two spies for them to show her *hesed* in saving her life. She said, "I have dealt kindly with you. Will you deal kindly with me?"

Hesed in the Bible

The Hebrew word חֶסֶד, which is transliterated as *checed* or *hesed*, is a masculine noun pronounced kheh'•sed. It's found 248 times in the King James translation of Old Testament, with the first reference in Genesis 19 and the last in Zechariah 7:9.[4]

Hesed is difficult to translate into just a single English word. Our English translations often use the words mercy, kindness, lovingkindness, goodness, kindly, merciful, and steadfast love.[5] The majority of times that *hesed* is mentioned in the Old Testament, it refers to God's character and His covenant with His people.[6] At other times, it refers to human relationships and implies loving our neighbor with acts of love and service. As the people of God, we are to do justice, to love kindness (*hesed*), and to walk humbly with our God (Mic. 6:8).[7]

Over half of the references to *hesed* occur within the book of Psalms, with the word showing up more than 100 times.[8] Psalm 136 in particular praises God for His steadfast love twenty-six times, once in each of its verses.

In just a few instances, *hesed* is used in a negative light and is translated as pity, reproach, or a wicked thing (Job 6:14; Ps. 57:3; Prov. 14:34; Lev. 20:17).[9]

In his commentary on this passage, Matthew Henry says:

> Those who truly believe the divine revelation concerning the ruin of sinners, and the grant of the heavenly land to God's Israel, will give diligence to flee from the wrath to come, and to lay hold of eternal life, by joining themselves to God and His people.[3]

That's exactly what Rahab did. The arrival of these men to Rahab's house was like someone throwing out a life preserver to her. She knew that unless they showed her mercy, she would perish. Though it cost her everything of earthly value and comfort, Rahab found that the *hesed* love of God is enough.

Describe a time in your life when you felt like you were drowning. How did God's faithful love rescue you then?

_____

_____

_____

_____

_____

_____

Psalm 136 mentions the steadfast love (or *hesed*) in each of its twenty-six verses. Read this passage and thank the Lord for how He has shown *hesed* to you.

Day 5: *Crying Out for Others*

Read Ezekiel 3:17–19.

In Joshua 2:12, who else did Rahab ask the spies to spare?

_____

_____

_____

_____

We don't know how Rahab communicated this news to her family. Did she have to plead with them to come into her house where they would be safe? Did they also believe the stories about God because of what Rahab told them? We don't know. However, Rahab had a sense of urgency. She knew her family was in danger and that this was their only hope. So, she had to tell them of the rescue that was available to them.

Ezekiel 3:17–19 gives us a word picture of the responsibility we have to share the gospel with others. Draw a picture of what this passage describes.

How was Rahab a "watchman" for her family?

_____

_____

_____

Isaiah 52:7–8 gives us another picture of being the bearer of good news. What details does this passage add to the image above? Add it to your picture.

Even though Rahab's faith was new, it was genuine. What evidence have we seen so far in our study that proves Rahab's faith was real?

_____

_____

_____

One evidence of genuine faith is that God gives us a concern for others to experience the Lord's lovingkindness and salvation. In his sermon entitled "Rahab's Faith," pastor and author Charles Spurgeon said, "Unless we desire others to taste the benefits we have enjoyed, we are either inhuman monsters or outrageous hypocrites; I think the last is most likely."[10]

The Lord's mercy is so good! Wouldn't we want others to taste and experience it too?

If you've been a Christ-follower for a long time, take some time to reflect on what it was like to live without the hope of Christ and ask the Lord to give you a deeper passion for the lost.

Make a list of the people in your life that you desire to come to know Christ.

_____

_____

_____

Are you praying regularly for the redemption of your family members? While you can't save them or even make them believe, you can cry out to God for their salvation, just as Rahab cried out to the two spies to save her family.

_____

_____

_____

In the book of Acts we read the story of a man who, like Rahab, came to faith and then immediately shared the news with his family.

Read the account of the Philippian jailer recorded in Acts 16:25–34.

How do we know that this man shared his faith in God with his family? What were the results?

_____

_____

_____

_____

_____

_____

The hope we have in Christ is not meant to be hidden. Our lost friends and family desperately need to know about the salvation available to them through Jesus. Go back to the list of family members you made above. Add any friends, coworkers, or neighbors who come to mind. Then pray for an opportunity like those God gave to Rahab and the Philippian jailer to point them to your redeeming God.

Red Thread
VERSE

Hesed. Steadfast love. Lovingkindness. It's why God saves His people from judgment. It's the reason the thread of redemption keeps going through the fabric of history. God showed His lovingkindness to the people of Israel, Abraham and Isaac's descendants, very clearly one night. They had been slaves for 400 years in Egypt, and in a mighty act of love and power, the Lord rescued them through ten plagues on their oppressors. *Frogs, boils, flies, ugh.* But the last plague required something of the Israelites: active faith. They had to obey God's command in order to be saved.

> "They shall take some of the blood [of a lamb] and put it on the two doorposts and the lintel of the houses . . . where you are. And when I see the blood, I will pass over you, and no plague will befall you to destroy you, when I strike the land of Egypt." (EX. 12:7, 13)

Our Red Thread Verse reminds us that just as Rahab was rescued by the red sign hanging out her window, the Israelites had been rescued years before by having a red sign on their doors. The plague of judgment passed over them. Both experienced God's *hesed;* both were redeemed. Yet you don't have to look much farther in the Bible *(ahem, we're looking at you, doubting spies)* to see that the sin problem wasn't completely taken care of yet. As we keep tracing the thread of redemption, one may wonder, *All this blood . . . and yet . . . where is that promised salvation?* It's coming in our story! Just keep following the scarlet trail.

Spend time meditating on and memorizing the following verse this week:

"Come now, let us reason together, says the Lord: though your sins are like scarlet, they shall be as white as snow; though they are red like crimson, they shall become like wool."

ISAIAH 1:18

Week 4
THE SCARLET CORD

Big Idea: THE SCARLET CORD IN JOSHUA 2 REPRESENTS GOD'S REDEEMING LOVE.

The Bayeux Tapestry is an incredible work of art. Located in the town of Bayeux in Normandy, France, this embroidered cloth stretches 230 feet long by twenty inches high. When you first stand in front of this large textile design comprised of nine panels of linen, it's easy to focus on the big picture, to marvel at the rich colors. Take a step closer for a better look, however, and you'll find the intricate needlework is woven with symbols and emblems that tell a much larger story—that of the Battle of Hastings and the Norman conquest of England.[1]

In Joshua 2, Rahab hangs a scarlet cord, or red thread, out her window as a signal for the approaching Israelite army that she and her household would be spared. Taken by itself, this thread represents Rahab's deliverance from the destruction of Jericho. However, if we take a step closer for a better look at the overall picture of God's Word, we find this thread intentionally woven throughout the different books, chapters, and verses of God's story of redemption.

This week, we'll take a closer look at that scarlet cord and find it was no coincidence the spies requested that Rahab hang it out her window. Through this single cord, we'll find an awesome image of our great redeeming God. As we trace the red thread throughout Scripture, we'll discover an overall picture of the blood of Jesus Christ that saves us from all sin.

Day 1: *A Sign of Obedience*

Read Joshua 2:12–21.

How do the men respond to Rahab's plea for mercy (v. 14)?

_____

_____

_____

List the four conditions Rahab needed to keep in order for the oath to be binding.

_____ (v. 18)

_____ (v. 18)

_____ (v. 19)

_____ (v. 20)

What did Rahab do after the spies left that shows she took them at their word (v. 21)?

_____

_____

_____

_____

_____

There's a sense of urgency in this passage. There was nothing more important for her to do. Through her actions, Rahab gives us an example of what true obedience to the Lord looks like: she obeyed *all the way and right away.*

What does disobedience of God ultimately reveal about our trust of God?

_____

_____

_____

Think of a time when you obeyed something the Lord asked you to do. What was the result?

_____

_____

_____

Think of a time when you disobeyed or delayed obeying something the Lord asked you to do. What was the result?

_____

_____

_____

_____

Rahab's act of obedience publicly showed her faith. When she hung the scarlet cord out of her window on the city wall, it could be seen by anyone who approached Jericho. As you think about the following people from Scripture and how they obeyed the Lord, describe how their obedience was visible for others to see.

Abraham
(GEN. 12:1-9; 22:1-19)

Esther
(EST. 4:8-5:8)

Mary
(LUKE 1:26-56)

Paul
(ACTS 9; 16:6-10)

How can visible acts of obedience to the Lord impact others around us?

_____

_____

_____

Is there something you know God wants you to do but you have hesitated? Write out a prayer confessing your weak faith and asking the Lord to help you step out and obey Him.

_____

_____

_____

_____

_____

_____

Day 2: *A Symbol of the Blood*

Read Isaiah 1:18.

When the spies made their agreement with Rahab, their first condition had to do with the cord they used to escape with: "Behold, when we come into the land, you shall tie this scarlet cord in the window through which you let us down" (Josh. 2:18).

Why do you think the spies requested this particular color?

_____

_____

_____

_____

God doesn't waste any details in His Word. He chose the color scarlet, or red, on purpose. We will learn why later in our study.

Notice what was missing in the conditions the spies gave to Rahab: they didn't say that in order to be rescued, she first needed to clean up her act. They met her where she was at and offered her a chance to be rescued.

Have you ever felt that in order for God to come to your rescue, you need to first get your life in order?

_____

_____

_____

According to Ephesians 1:4, when did Christ choose us?

_____

_____

According to Romans 5:8, when did Christ die for us?

_____

_____

Were we able to "clean up our acts" or rid ourselves of sinful tendencies before God moved toward us with love and grace?

_____

_____

_____

_____

How does knowing that God meets us where we're at and offers us His forgiveness change that thinking?

_____

_____

_____

_____

Read Isaiah 1:18 below and underline the phrases used to describe our sins.

> "Come now, let us reason together, says the LORD:
> though your sins are like scarlet,
>   they shall be as white as snow;
> though they are red like crimson,
>   they shall become like wool."

What color is used to represent sin in this passage?

_____

_____

Go back and circle the words in Isaiah 1:18 that describe how our sins appear when we repent and receive Christ as our Savior.

Write a brief description or draw an image of the word picture in this passage and how it affects you.

The innocent Son of God shed His blood for sinners, and His blood is on our hands. Our sins are as scarlet. They are red like crimson. Yet God promises, "You can be white as snow."

Much like the famed scarlet letter, scarlet can be a symbol of the sin, guilt, and shame that so many of us wear. Yet it doesn't have to be. Scarlet can represent something else: our means of salvation.

The Color Scarlet in the Bible

The word "scarlet" occurs nearly fifty times in the Bible, six of which are in the New Testament.

Scarlet was one of the colors used for the curtains in the tabernacle (Ex. 26:31). It was also one of the colors of the garments of the high priest (Ex. 28:5–15). Scarlet robes were used to symbolize royalty (2 Sam. 1:24; Jer. 4:30; Rev. 17:4) and were also worn by warriors (Nah. 2:3).[2]

When Tamar delivered twins, one of the babies stuck his hand out of the womb first. The midwife tied a scarlet thread around his wrist (Gen. 38:27–30). Scarlet thread is mentioned as part of the rites of cleansing the leper (Lev. 14) and of the purification ceremony of burning the red heifer (Num. 19:6).

And of course, Rahab hung a scarlet cord out her window to remind the Israelite army to spare her household (Josh. 2).

In Matthew 27:28, the soldiers put a scarlet robe on Jesus in order to mock him. In Isaiah, God describes our sins as "scarlet" (1:18). And the Proverbs 31 woman clothed her family in scarlet (Prov. 31:21), which represented high quality clothing that kept her family warm in winter.[3]

Next to each of the following references, write down what covers and washes away our sin.

EPHESIANS 2:13

1 JOHN 1:7

REVELATION 1:4-5

Do you still live under guilt or shame over past sin that you've confessed to the Lord? How can you remind yourself that Jesus' blood takes away your sin and makes you white as snow (Isa. 1:18)? Journal your answer below.

_____

_____

_____

_____

Day 3: *A Picture of Passover*

Read Exodus 12:1–32.

As we learned from our Red Thread Verse last week, the red thread in Rahab's story points to another significant event in Israel's history—the Passover.

In the table below, list similarities between the Passover recorded in Exodus 12 and what you've learned about Rahab's story so far.

PASSOVER	RAHAB'S STORY

According to Joshua 5:10, the Israelites celebrated the Passover right before they invaded Jericho. God, in His Providence, linked the timing of this sacred celebration to Rahab's rescue and His judgment upon the Canaanites.

Just as the Israelites had to be in their homes during the Passover, Rahab and her family had to be in her house when the attack came upon Jericho. Instead of blood on the doorposts to mark her house for salvation, Rahab had a scarlet cord hanging in the window. When the Israelites came to take over the land, they saw the red cord. While they judged all the other houses on behalf of the Lord, the righteous Judge, they passed over Rahab's home. She and her family were spared, just as the Israelites had been at the first Passover.

According to Romans 3:10 and 23, who deserves judgment?

_____

_____

_____

_____

God's judgment is ultimately meant to showcase His salvation. What have we been saved from? His righteous judgment.

For each story, list how God provided both judgment and salvation.

	GOD'S JUDGMENT	GOD'S SALVATION
Passover		
Rahab		

Both the Passover and the story of Rahab point us to the gospel. Jesus, the spotless, blameless Lamb of God, was sacrificed for us. He died in our place on the cross, taking the penalty we deserve, so that God will pass over us in His judgment. We have been saved from spiritual death and separation from God by Christ's blood, our scarlet cord.

End today's study by reflecting upon the description of Jesus in Isaiah 53.

> He [Jesus] was despised and rejected by men,
>   a man of sorrows and acquainted with grief;
> and as one from whom men hide their faces
>   he was despised, and we esteemed him not.
>
> Surely he has borne our griefs
>   and carried our sorrows;
> yet we esteemed him stricken,
>   smitten by God, and afflicted.
> But he was pierced for our transgressions;
>   he was crushed for our iniquities;
> upon him was the chastisement that brought us peace,
>   and with his wounds we are healed.
> All we like sheep have gone astray;
>   we have turned—every one—to his own way;
> and the LORD has laid on him
>   the iniquity of us all. (vv. 3-6)

Day 4: *A Reminder of the Covenant*

Read John 1:17.

Not only is the scarlet cord a powerful and important symbol of sin and forgiveness, it's also a sign of the covenant (a.k.a. agreement) between the spies and Rahab.

Look up the word "covenant" in both a standard dictionary and a Bible dictionary or encyclopedia. Write out a definition in your own words below.

_____

_____

_____

Covenant = A binding agreement + God's faithfulness in Jesus to keep it

What does Psalm 25:14 reveal about the covenant of God?

_____

_____

_____

Through His Word, God has revealed His covenant agreement with us. One example can be found in 1 John 1:9. In the passage below, underline what our part of the agreement is. Circle what God's part of the agreement is.

> If we confess our sins, he is faithful and just to forgive us our sins and to cleanse us from all unrighteousness.

How did the scarlet cord represent the covenant between Rahab and the spies?

_____

_____

_____

Throughout Scripture, God used various physical signs to remind people of His promises. For each passage below, draw a line to the matching sign that God used.

Genesis 9:12–17   Broken Bread/Poured Out Wine

Genesis 17:9–14   Blood of Oxen

Exodus 24:3–8   Rainbow

Luke 22:19–20   Circumcision

In Rahab's case, the scarlet cord was the sign that she had entered into a covenant with the spies and made a profession of faith in God. By hanging it outside her window, she expressed her desire to be saved from God's judgment.

The spies had promised to preserve her life; however, she still would have perished if she had not demonstrated her faith by hanging the scarlet cord. Her life depended on that scarlet thread.

Rahab was not placing her faith in the scarlet cord itself but in all it represented. Ultimately, her faith was in God to save her. **It's not the physical symbol or sign that saves us—God alone can save.**

Look up Romans 2:25–29.

What symbol does this passage warn against relying on for salvation?

_____

_____

Now look at Deuteronomy 10:12–16 and 30:6. What did God intend for this rite to symbolize spiritually?

_____

_____

Why might it be easy for people to put their faith in a physical sign rather than in the One whom it represents?

_____

_____

What good things are you prone to trust more than God? (Circle all that apply).

Baptism	Clothing	Connections
Status	Media Choices	Man's Approval
Communion	Family Heritage	Talents
Church Membership	Good Works	Productivity
Personal Quiet Time	Money	

Add any others that come to mind to the list above.

In Deuteronomy 30:15–18, God made a covenant with the Israelites that He would bless them and protect them if they would obey Him and keep His law. God kept His promise, but the Israelites could not—just as we cannot perfectly stick to God's standards of holiness. So, God made a new covenant with us.

God made a new covenant with us through the blood of His Son to forgive our sins and restore a relationship with us. Through Jesus, there is hope for us who have sinned, who are covenant breakers.

Look up the following passages and write a description of the new covenant next to each one.

JOHN 1:17

HEBREWS 8:8–12

HEBREWS 9:11–15

Revisit 1 John 1:9. What is our part of the covenant?

_____

_____

It sounds simple enough, but because we are sinners we won't always keep up our end of the bargain. God's covenant agreement to forgive and accept His children depends on His faithfulness, not our perfection.

Covenant ≠ us keeping the agreement perfectly.

How have you seen God demonstrate grace in this area in your own life?

_____

_____

_____

_____

Day 5: *Woven Throughout God's Word*

Read Ephesians 1:7.

In Rahab's life, the scarlet cord represents:

• Her sin

• Her obedience

• Her faith

• God's forgiveness of her sin

Rahab's story reveals that the scarlet cord is significant for all of us.

From the first century on, commentators and church fathers have seen this scarlet cord as a symbol of the blood of Jesus. It represents the mercy of God that redeems us from the guilt and shame of sin. It's the blood of Jesus Christ that is our only hope of salvation.

This scarlet cord runs all the way through the Bible. Today, our lesson is going to be a little different as we look at various Scripture passages to see how that red thread is woven throughout all of God's Word.

First, let's look at the Old Testament. Look up each passage and fill in the chart to help you find the scarlet cord in each one.

PASSAGE	WHO SINNED IN THIS PASSAGE (IF ANYONE)?	WHAT DIED IN THIS PASSAGE?	HOW DO YOU SEE GOD RESPONDING?
Genesis 3:1–21	Adam and Eve	An animal	Covering them with skins
Genesis 4:1–16			
Genesis 22:1–18			
Exodus 12:1–13, 21–28			
Leviticus 16:11–16			

All of those Old Testament symbols were merely shadows that pointed toward the blood redemption of Jesus Christ, the sinless Lamb of God.

Hebrews 9:22 tells us, "Under the law almost everything is purified with blood, and without the shedding of blood there is no forgiveness of sins." And then in Hebrews 10:4, it says, "It is impossible for the blood of bulls and goats to take away sins."

Animal sacrifices couldn't forgive sin. God would forgive the people who brought the sacrifices because of their faith in His promise of forgiveness and the coming Savior. Like the scarlet cord hanging outside Rahab's window, Christ's cross is a symbol that reminds us that salvation has come.

Now let's look at some examples of the scarlet cord—Jesus' blood—throughout the New Testament. Again, write how it shows up in each passage.

PASSAGE	WHAT DOES JESUS' BLOOD DO IN THIS PASSAGE?
Matthew 26:27–28	Makes a new covenant, brings forgiveness of sins.
Ephesians 1:7	
Hebrews 9:12	
1 John 1:7	
Revelation 1:5	
Revelation 5:9–10	
Revelation 19:11–13	

The shed blood of Christ brings God's forgiveness for all our sins—all of them! The ones everyone knows about and the ones no one knows about. They are all gone, through the blood of Christ who washes away our sin.

However, there's a condition—we must put our faith in Christ. Like Rahab threw a cord out of her window out of trust, to be saved we must turn toward Christ, acknowledge that we are needy, and confess that He is the only One who can save us.

Have you tied the scarlet cord in the window of your life by putting your faith in Him?

_____

_____

_____

_____

God's wrath is coming. The walls of this world's kingdom are going to tumble down (2 Peter 3:10). Those who have rejected the truth of God's saving love will be destroyed. They will be judged. Will you be spared? If you are, it won't be because you:

• Were good.
• Were a church member.
• Didn't commit certain sins.
• Helped others.

None of that will count. **If you are spared from God's wrath, it will be for one reason alone—because, like Rahab, you trusted the one true God to save you.**

Red Thread
VERSE

This week, we learned about the symbolism of the scarlet cord. Did you notice a Scripture passage that kept coming up again and again? It's also our Red Thread Verse for the week.

> "What to me is the multitude of your sacrifices?
>   says the LORD;
> I have had enough of burnt offerings of rams
>   and the fat of well-fed beasts;
> I do not delight in the blood of bulls,
>   or of lambs, or of goats. . . .
> Come now, let us reason together, says the LORD:
> though your sins are like scarlet,
>   they shall be as white as snow;
> though they are red like crimson,
>   they shall become like wool." (ISA. 1:11, 18)

After years and years of sacrifices—at Passover, in the Promised Land, in the temple Solomon built . . . the people of Israel's hearts still hadn't changed. They were obedient outwardly, bringing cows and sheep and goats to the priests year after year after year. But they hadn't turned to the Lord for grace. Yet He was there, with *hesed,* inviting them to His salvation. This is key. It is God's grace that rescues us, not our ability to obey or bring sacrifices. It's the God behind the symbols and signs that brings redemption! But *how!?* Perhaps you feel like the Israelites in Isaiah's day may have. *We've read and read and read about this redemption to come. We know who God is and what He requires of us, but we can't measure up! How can we be made white as snow?* Next week's Red Thread Verse will *finally* answer that question. The meaning of the thread of God's redemption will be revealed.

Spend time meditating on and memorizing the following verse this week:

God is our REFUGE & STRENGTH, a very present HELP in trouble.

PSALM 46:1

Week 5

THE BIG PICTURE

Big Idea: WE CAN ALWAYS TRUST IN GOD'S PROMISES.

Georges Seurat's famous painting "A Sunday Afternoon on the Island of La Grande Jatte" features a large landscape of people relaxing in a Parisian park. When you stand back and admire the almost seven- by ten-foot canvas, you'll find among the bright colors three dogs, eight boats, and forty-eight people (plus a monkey!).[1]

Get up close, however, and your eyes will blur as you see millions of dots—the artistic technique of pointillism. This masterpiece was never meant to be viewed only inches away. The artist used tiny, seemingly insignificant dots of paint to create a larger, grander image that tells a story you can only truly see when you stand back and look at the entire picture.

Similarly, when we're up close to the events happening in the here and now, we can't see the big picture of what God is doing. We only see the little dots of time and space that we occupy at this moment. But God is omniscient; He knows everything. Our point of view is limited. God has a wide-angle lens. He sees the whole picture that He is painting.

As we will learn this week, even when we don't understand what God is doing in our lives, we can still trust in His promises.

Day 1: *Waiting for Rescue*

Read Joshua 2:16–25.

Rahab took the spies' conditions for her salvation at their word. How do we know that the spies trusted Rahab in return (vv. 16, 22)?

_____

_____

_____

Write a brief description of the report the spies brought back to Joshua (v. 24).

_____

_____

_____

_____

Back in Jericho, we don't know exactly what Rahab was doing, as the Bible doesn't give us specifics. However, in order to fulfill her oath to the spies, she had to do four things:

1. Hang the scarlet cord out her window
2. Gather her family into her home
3. Stay in the house
4. Not tell anyone else

Read Joshua 6:22–25. How do we know that Rahab fulfilled the ssecond, third, and fourth parts of her oath?

_____

_____

_____

Put yourself in Rahab's shoes. What would it take for you to tell your family about the coming judgment? Circle the words below.

foolishness

courage

love

IMPULSIVENESS

FAITH

persuasion   risk

judgmentalism

There is one more thing Rahab must have done after the spies' departure—she had to wait. After she gathered her family into her home, they all waited, with the scarlet cord hanging outside the window, until the Israelites returned.

Why do you think it was necessary for Rahab and her family to stay in the house at all times?

_____

_____

_____

Rahab didn't know how long she would have to wait. She didn't know what was going on across the river at the Israelite camp. All she knew was that she had to wait in her house, in faith, with her family and be ready whenever the Israelites came to conquer Jericho.

Write down some words to describe what it must have been like inside Rahab's home as they waited.

_____

_____

_____

_____

Today, we're also called to be ready for something that could happen at any time—the return of our Lord Jesus Christ. The return of Christ could happen at any time, so we need to be prepared. Look up the following passages and fill in the chart below.

PASSAGE	WHAT WILL CHRIST'S RETURN LOOK LIKE?	HOW SHOULD THAT IMPACT OUR DAILY LIVES?
Matthew 24:36–50		
Matthew 25:1–13		
Mark 13:32–37		
2 Peter 3:8–13		

As you wait for Jesus' return, ask yourself, *Am I ready?* Close today's study by meditating on Luke 21:27–28 below, and pray that you would live your life in light of eternity and His ultimate rescue.

> "They will see the Son of Man coming in a cloud with power and great glory. Now when these things begin to take place, straighten up and raise your heads, because your redemption is drawing near."

Day 2: *A Different Perspective*

Read Joshua 6:1–20.

When we hear the account of the fall of Jericho, it's usually told from Joshua's perspective or that of the children of Israel. Today, however, we're going to think about this familiar story from Rahab's perspective.

Write out Joshua 6:1 below and underline the phrases that describe what was going on in Jericho at this time.

_____

_____

_____

_____

Jericho was in a state of siege, and the enemy hadn't even appeared. The people were terrified because they had heard what God had done in the past. No one was allowed in or out of the city. Tensions were high.

Since Rahab lived in the city walls, it's conceivable to think she could have watched from her window as she waited for the Israelites to return.

Write a brief description of what she would have seen and heard when the Israelite army finally did appear (vv. 8–11).

_____

_____

_____

_____

Circle any emotions Rahab might have been feeling as she watched the Israelites march around the city.

doubt

sadness *fear*

CONFUSION

curiosity apprehension

SKEPTICISM

disappointment

anticipation *excitement*

Rahab probably had mixed emotions when she saw the Israelite army approach Jericho, as she thought about what was going to happen to all the people she knew and had grown up with. She knew they were all going to die since they had rejected God. But perhaps she also had an inner sense of assurance that she and her family were going to be spared.

What do you think Rahab thought when the army marched around the city in silence and left?

_____

_____

_____

What Rahab saw out her window was only a small part of the bigger picture. She wasn't aware of God's instructions to Joshua in Joshua 6:2–5. While she had faith that God had given the Israelites the land, she didn't know how that was going to happen.

Just like Rahab, we can only see "out our window." As we look at the troubling events in our lives and our world, we're looking at it from a limited and finite perspective. We don't have the whole picture.

Look up the following verses. What do they tell us about God's plan for the big picture of our lives?

GENESIS 50:20

JEREMIAH 29:11

ROMANS 8:28-29

Looking back, how can you see God's bigger purpose in events in your life that you didn't understand at the time?

_____
_____
_____
_____
_____

How has God used those things to shape you into the image of Christ?

_____
_____
_____
_____

Match the following verses with the correct reference.

John 13:7

> For my thoughts are not your thoughts,
>> neither are your ways my ways,
>> declares the LORD.
> For as the heavens are higher than the earth,
>> so are my ways higher than your ways
>> and my thoughts than your thoughts.

Psalm 37:10–11

> Jesus answered him, "What I am doing you do not understand now, but afterward you will understand."

Isaiah 55:8–9

> In just a little while, the wicked will be no more;
>> though you look carefully at his place,
>> he will not be there.
> But the meek shall inherit the land
>> and delight themselves in abundant peace.

What do these verses tell us about the difference between our and God's perspective?

_____

_____

_____

_____

In light of this, what does 2 Corinthians 5:6–7 tell us about how we should live?

_____

_____

_____

_____

The Walls of Jericho

Jericho was a heavily fortified city built on a mount, called a "tel" in archaeological terms. It was surrounded by a steep hill or embankment that had a stone retaining wall at its base. This wall measured between twelve to fifteen feet high at the base of the city. On top of that retaining wall was a mud brick wall six feet thick and twenty to twenty-six feet tall.[3]

Then, at the top of the embankment above the first retaining wall was another mud brick wall, which stretched forty-six feet above the outside barrier. This is the fortress that towered over the Israelites as they marched around Jericho each day.[4]

When German archaeologists Ernst Sellin and Carl Watzinger did their excavations of Jericho in the early 1900s, they found these double walls, as well as a short segment of the lower city wall that was still standing. All of the other walls had crumbled, but a small section remained. In this part of the city, the archeologists also found houses built against the outer wall that had not been destroyed.[5]

Since we don't have the same perspective as God, we need to walk in this world by faith, trusting that He can see things that we don't see. **If we could see what God sees and know what He knows, our hearts would be at peace.**

As we end today, take time to reflect upon the following poem, which speaks of God's view of the bigger picture and His master plan for our lives.

The Weaver

My life is but a weaving
Between my God and me;
I cannot choose the colors
He worketh steadily.

Sometimes He weaveth sorrow,
And I in foolish pride
Forget He sees the upper,
And I the under side.

Not til the loom is silent
And the shuttles cease to fly,
Shall God unroll the canvas
And explain the reason why.

The dark threads are as needful
In the Weaver's skillful hand
As the threads of gold and silver
In the pattern He has planned.

He knows, He loves, He cares,
Nothing this truth can dim;
He gives His very best to those
Who chose to walk with Him.[2]

Day 3: *Trusting His Promises*

Read Luke 19:9–10.

As Rahab watched the Israelites march around the city, she might have been tempted to doubt that she and her family would be saved. All she had to rely on was the word of two strangers who had stayed in her home. They promised that God was going to give them the land and that they would spare her and her family's lives when they returned.

When have you been tempted to doubt God's working in your life?

_____

_____

How do you remind yourself (or others) to trust God when it feels like you're in a war?

_____

_____

_____

In Luke 19, Jesus reveals to Zacchaeus about why He came. What was that reason?

_____

_____

Much like the spies who sought out Rahab and explained how she could be saved, Jesus sought out the lost to let us know how we could escape the coming destruction.

Use the chart below to list other similarities between the spies' visit to Rahab's home and Jesus' coming to live among us.

SPIES' VISIT TO RAHAB	JESUS' VISIT TO OUR WORLD

Jesus made an oath before He left this earth, just as the spies had to Rahab. He promised that one day He would return. He didn't tell us how long it would be or when He would come back. He just promised that He *would* come back.

As we wait for that day, sometimes it looks like God isn't doing anything about the evil in this world. Some days we may be tempted to wonder if He will really come back for us.

Though things may look bleak, we can trust God's promises.

Write out John 14:3 below.

_____

_____

_____

_____

_____

How does this passage give you hope as you wait?

_____

_____

_____

_____

What are some other promises from God's Word that give you hope and assurance? Write them below.

_____

_____

_____

_____

How did the people listed in Hebrews 11 trust in the Lord's promises even when they didn't see the outcome?

_____

_____

_____

How does their example encourage you as you trust in God's promises today?

_____

_____

_____

Remember the emotions we looked at yesterday? God sees each of those feelings and can help you in them with His love and compassion. His promises are true for *you*, whether you are afraid, joyful, or disappointed.

To finish out today's study, fill in the chart below. Then, choose the promise that best fits your current situation, and write it somewhere you can look at it often—on a chalkboard, sticky note, your bathroom mirror, etc.

WHEN I AM FEELING . . .	I CAN TRUST GOD'S PROMISE . . .	THAT HE WILL . . .
Skepticism	Ps. 111:7-8	
Fear	Ps. 23:4	
Anticipation	Ps. 34:5	
Excitement	Col. 3:23-24	
Curiosity	Jer. 29:13	
Apprehension	Prov. 3:5-6	
Sadness	John 16:20	
Doubt	Isa. 41:10	
Confusion	James 1:5	
Disappointment	1 Peter 3:12	

Day 4: *Judgment and Salvation*

Read Joshua 6:15–27.

As children in Sunday school, we might have sung about the battle of Jericho and how the "walls came a-tumbling down." Sometimes when stories are as familiar as a childhood song, we can easily miss some important truths the Lord wants to teach us through it.

What famous miracle does this passage contain?

_____

_____

_____

When the walls of Jericho fell down, it wasn't just a judgment upon the people of Canaan; it was a foreshadowing of the judgment that is coming on this sinful world someday.

Read Joshua 6:22–23 below, and underline what happened to Rahab and her family after the defeat of Jericho.

> To the two men who had spied out the land, Joshua said, "Go into the prostitute's house and bring out from there the woman and all who belong to her, as you swore to her." So the young men who had been spies went in and brought out Rahab and her father and mother and brothers and all who belonged to her. And they brought all her relatives and put them outside the camp of Israel.

Why was it necessary for Rahab to be put outside the Israelite camp? Look up the following passages for insight.

NUMBERS 5:1-4

NUMBERS 12:14

DEUTERONOMY 23:9-14

Rahab and her family had to be outside the camp, at least temporarily, because they were ceremonially unclean. They needed to be cleansed and purified according to Jewish law before they could join the rest of the Israelites.

This gives us a beautiful picture of what Jesus did for us. Hebrews 13:12 says, "Jesus also suffered outside the gate in order to sanctify the people through his own blood." When Jesus took the sins of the world on Himself, He became unclean. He went to the lowest place—being separated from God and His people—to raise us up and make us clean. He went "outside the camp" so to speak, to bring us in to the people of God. He "was delivered up for our trespasses and raised for our justification" (Rom. 4:25). When He was resurrected, Jesus overcame the pollution of sin that put Him outside the camp, and when we trust Him for salvation, we are made pure and alive in Him.

Read Joshua 6:20–21. What happened to the rest of the people of Jericho?

_____

_____

_____

Do you feel that the judgment on Jericho is fair or unfair? Why?

_____

_____

_____

_____

Rahab was no less a sinner than anybody else in Jericho, yet God gave her faith and spared her life to show His mercy.

Look up the following passages. Next to each reference, write what each one teaches about God's desire for humanity.

EZEKIEL 18:23

MATTHEW 23:37

2 PETER 3:9

1 TIMOTHY 2:3-4

Because God is holy and cannot stand sin, He must judge the wicked—either through eternal judgment in hell or through Jesus taking our judgment on Himself. The difference is God's mercy. The inclination of His heart is to show mercy toward sinners who will repent and believe.

We've all sinned and fall short of God's holiness. We all experience the pain, sorrow, and suffering of living in a sinful world. But Jesus came to offer us redemption.

At the cross, where Jesus drank the full cup of sorrow and pain that every person in the world through all of history deserved, judgment and salvation met. They came together so that the world might be able to receive forgiveness, comfort, and healing.

Read the following verses below and underline the Lord's promise for the future when we trust in Him.

> "Truly, truly, I say to you, you will weep and lament, but the world will rejoice. You will be sorrowful, but your sorrow will turn into joy. . . . So also you have sorrow now, but I will see you again, and your hearts will rejoice, and no one will take your joy from you." (JOHN 16:20, 22)
>
> And the ransomed of the LORD shall return
>   and come to Zion with singing;
> everlasting joy shall be upon their heads;
>   they shall obtain gladness and joy,
>   and sorrow and sighing shall flee away. (ISA. 51:11)

It's an awesome thing to think that God took our sorrows on Himself. And because He did, here's the incredible news: **For those who trust in Christ, one day God will turn all our sorrows into joy.**

To conclude today's study, read the verses below and personalize them with your own name.

He was despised and rejected by _____,
    a man of sorrows and acquainted with grief;
and as one from whom _____ hide[s] [her face]
    he was despised, and _____ esteemed him not.
Surely he has borne _____ griefs

and carried _____ sorrows;

yet _____ esteemed him stricken,

   smitten by God, and afflicted.

But he was pierced for _____ transgressions;

   he was crushed for _____ iniquities;

upon him was the chastisement that brought _____ peace,

   and with his wounds _____ [is] healed.

_____ like sheep [has] gone astray;

_____ [has] turned . . . to _____ own way;

and the Lord has laid on him

   the iniquity of _____. (Isa. 53:3–6)

For _____ [has] sinned and fall[s] short of the glory of God (Rom. 3:23).

Day 5: *He's Our Refuge*

Read Psalm 46.

When the Israelites marched around Jericho, Rahab knew she wasn't going to find refuge in the fortress of the city walls. Although she didn't know a lot about God, she looked to Him and His people to protect her.

Today, we have spiritual advantages that Rahab never had—we have the cross and we have the Bible. Yet there are many people who have heard the truth over and over again but have never been willing to repent of their sins and place their trust in Jesus.

What are some things that people look to for comfort and help when they're suffering?

_____

_____

_____

_____

_____

_____

Look up the following verses. What does each one teach will happen if we don't look to Christ for refuge from our sin?

JOHN 3:18

ACTS 4:11-12

2 PETER 3:7

MATTHEW 13:40-42

Way before the time of Rahab, God had instructed Moses about providing specific places of refuge for people in trouble.

Read Numbers 35:9–12. What was the purpose of these cities of refuge? Who were they for?

_____

_____

_____

_____

_____

_____

Those who ran to one of the six cities of refuge could present his or her case to the elders. If he or she was found innocent, then they were allowed to stay in the city under their protection until the death of the high priest (v. 25).

Jesus is our place of refuge. This does not mean we will never be in physical danger. **There will never be a time when we'll be completely destroyed; He is our eternal safe place.**

Record Jesus' words found in Matthew 10:28.

_____

_____

_____

_____

Not only does Jesus offer us refuge from sin, He is also a refuge in times of trouble. He can give us stability, comfort, and peace during the hardships we experience in life.

Match each of the following passages with how it describes God as our refuge.

Psalm 46:1   Strong tower

Psalm 91:1–2   Perfect peace

Proverbs 18:10   Fortress

Isaiah 26:3   Help in time of trouble

We're all going to encounter trouble in our life. It is an inescapable reality in a fallen world. Sometimes those troubles are huge, like the army conquering Rahab's city. Other times, they're more chronic, creeping, and cumulative. Yet it's these circumstances that point us to our all-powerful God.

As you think about your current troubles, where are you turning for refuge?

_____

_____

_____

Are you trusting in anything or anyone other than God?

_____

_____

_____

As you end this week, take time to reflect on Psalm 46. Then rewrite it in your own words in the space below, asking Jesus to help you run to Him for shelter.

_____

_____

_____

_____

_____

_____

_____

_____

Red Thread
VERSE

This is the week we've been looking for this whole study! And this is the Red Thread Verse! This is the meaning of the thread of redemption:

> God shows his love for us in that while we were still sinners, Christ died for us. Since, therefore, we have now been justified by his blood, much more shall we be saved by him from the wrath of God. (ROM. 5:8-9)

Jesus *is* the thread of redemption. *He* is the one who fulfills all of God's promises and delivers us. When the walls come down in this world, everyone who is in Jesus' house is safe—forever. Our sins can be forgiven, our stories can be redeemed, our sorrows can finally turn to joy! How? The same way God's people have always been redeemed:

By God's grace—like Adam and Eve experienced (week 1).
Through God providing a substitute (Jesus)—like Isaac was rescued (week 2).
With faith in what God said—like the Israelites in Egypt had (week 3).
While turning to God for help—like the people in Isaiah's day needed to do (week 4).

God offers us His mercy through Jesus' death in our place. If we believe this, agree with Him that He is our hearts' and stories' only hope for redemption, and turn to Him to be rescued . . . we *will* be saved. If you've never done this, do it now! He is waiting to welcome you into His family, just like Rahab. *This* is the redemption we've been following for five weeks. Praise God! And next week, we'll find out where the thread ends. Hint: There's a happy ending coming!

Spend time meditating on and memorizing the following verse this week:

IF ANYONE IS IN CHRIST,
HE IS A *new* CREATION.
THE OLD HAS PASSED AWAY;
behold, the new has come.

2 CORINTHIANS 5:17

Week 6

A NEW IDENTITY

Big Idea: JESUS GIVES US A NEW IDENTITY WORTH CELEBRATING.

It's not easy to change your identity. You need to fill out multiple documents and attend several legal hearings. Then you need to change your name on everything and get a new Social Security number! Experts also recommend that you get in touch with law enforcement.

Whether we ever go through this formal process or not, most of us have the desire to put our past behind us. We want our mistakes to be wiped clean and to start anew. To do that, however, our lives need to completely change. In essence, we need a new identity. In this final week of our study, we'll see how that happened with Rahab—and how it can happen in our lives as well.

As we switch gears and study what the New Testament has to say about Rahab, we'll discover how God offers us a fresh start and new identity through His Son, Jesus, regardless of our past. But He doesn't only save us from past sin; He gives us the freedom to face the future without fear, to live out our faith in Him, and to have hope, no matter what comes. And He calls us to share our story so that others can experience the wonder of His amazing grace and have a new identity, too.

Day 1: *From Prostitute to Princess*

Read Matthew 1:1–17.

The first New Testament reference to Rahab takes place in the book of Matthew, which lists the genealogy of Jesus. Because the list is long, we might be tempted to skip all of these names, but if we do, we miss some deeper truths.

This list of names, most of which we're not familiar with and some of which we can hardly pronounce, reminds us of how important individuals are to God.

These names matter to God. They were a part of His plan of redemption. He knows just where we fit into His eternal plan and purposes and that where we fit is important to God.

As you read through these verses, do you recognize any of the names?

_____

_____

_____

_____

Abraham, Isaac, Jacob, David, Solomon . . . these are all names we might expect to find in the line of Christ: the patriarchs of the Jewish nation, a man after God's own heart, the wisest man to ever live.

Write out Matthew 1:5–6.

_____

_____

_____

_____

_____

_____

It was unusual in that day and age for women's names to be included in a genealogy, because typically the family line was traced through the men. Also, this was written in a culture where women were considered inferior.

What does the inclusion of women in Jesus' family tree tell us about how God views women?

_____

_____

_____

_____

Write down the names of the other women listed in the genealogy of Jesus.

_____

_____

_____

_____

Look up the passages in the table below and write a two- to three-word description of each woman listed.

Tamar	Genesis 38
Rahab	Joshua 2
Ruth	Ruth 1
Bathsheba (the wife of Uriah)	2 Samuel 11
Mary	Luke 1:26–38

What does the listing of these women tell us about God's character? Circle any words that apply.

angry unloving forgiving rescuer full of grace unapproachable merciful REDEEMER

Rahab is an incredible example of the grace of God at work. He gave Rahab a new identity, dealt with her past, and gave her freedom to face the future without fear.

Write a list of words to describe Rahab's new identity.

_____

_____

_____

Rahab wasn't just delivered and left outside the camp of the Israelites or enslaved or made a second-class citizen. She was richly blessed by God, grafted into a new family, and made a part of a new community of faith.

Read 1 Corinthians 1:27–29 below.

> God chose what is foolish in the world to shame the wise; God chose what is weak in the world to shame the strong; God chose what is low and despised in the world, even things that are not, to bring to nothing things that are, so that no human being might boast in the presence of God.

How do you see these verses reflected in the story of Rahab?

_____

_____

_____

Because she became part of the family of Jesus, the King of Kings, Rahab the Canaanite prostitute became Rahab the Jewish princess. What did she have to give up for her change of identity?

_____

_____

_____

What did she gain?

_____

_____

_____

_____

When we choose to follow Christ today, what do we have to give up?

_____

_____

_____

What do we gain?

_____

_____

_____

If God can change Rahab the prostitute into Rahab the Jewish princess, how can He transform your life?

To end today's study, use a red pen or marker to trace the red thread of redemption through the genealogy of Christ.

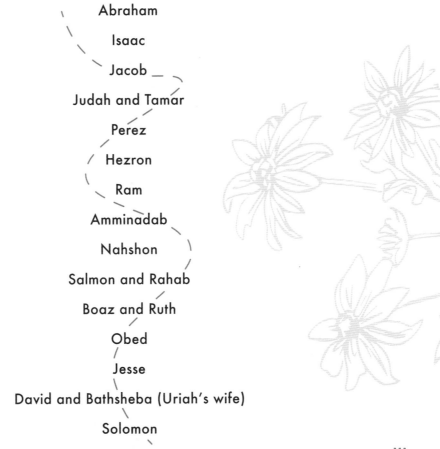

Abraham

Isaac

Jacob

Judah and Tamar

Perez

Hezron

Ram

Amminadab

Nahshon

Salmon and Rahab

Boaz and Ruth

Obed

Jesse

David and Bathsheba (Uriah's wife)

Solomon

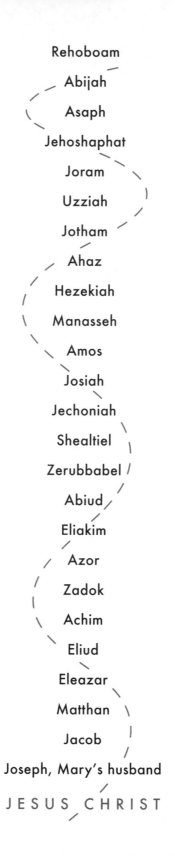

Rehoboam

Abijah

Asaph

Jehoshaphat

Joram

Uzziah

Jotham

Ahaz

Hezekiah

Manasseh

Amos

Josiah

Jechoniah

Shealtiel

Zerubbabel

Abiud

Eliakim

Azor

Zadok

Achim

Eliud

Eleazar

Matthan

Jacob

Joseph, Mary's husband

JESUS CHRIST

Day 2: *A Picture of the Gospel*

Read 2 Corinthians 5:17.

As we discussed yesterday, Rahab the prostitute became Rahab the Jewish princess. She married into the Jewish nation and became part of the lineage of Jesus Christ.

But that raises a question. In Deuteronomy 7:1–3, God gave the Israelites specific instructions about intermarriage with the Canaanites. What were they?

_____

_____

_____

Since Rahab was a Canaanite, why could she live in Israel and marry an Israelite? Because Rahab *wasn't* a Canaanite anymore. By faith she became an Israelite. She was a woman of faith in God, no longer a pagan.

Look up the verses below. How is Rahab's life a picture of what these verses are describing?

2 CORINTHIANS 5:17

EPHESIANS 2:19

If you are in Christ, you are not who you once were. You're a new creation. You have new identity papers. Your past sins are forgiven, and there's hope for your future.

Ultimately, what does Rahab's story tell us about who God is able to save?

_____

_____

_____

According to Galatians 3:10, we are _____ if we don't _____ by everything written in the _____ of the ___.

We're all Rahabs. We were all born rebellious against God. We are all prone to going our way and doing our own thing. Some have done it with sexual sin. Some have done it by substance abuse, drugs, and alcohol, and some have done it with pride and self-sufficiency and hypocrisy. We're all hopeless and helpless—apart from the grace of God and the scarlet cord, the blood of Jesus Christ, that was shed to pay for our sins.

No matter our past, we can be saved through Jesus Christ. No matter how hopelessly lost we might think others are, they can be saved as well.

Read Ephesians 2:8–9. Write it out in your own words.

_____

_____

_____

_____

Rahab's salvation was not based on her character or anything good that she had done. She lived in a wicked city and had a wicked life. She wasn't saved because of her goodness or because she had cleaned up her act. She was saved by the grace of God.

That's what the gospel is all about.

The Gospel = Abounding Sin & Super-Abounding Grace

Rahab's story also shows us the lengths God will go to redeem and rescue hopelessly lost sinners.

Why would God send the two spies into Jericho? How necessary was the information they gained from their trip to the conquest of the city?

_____

_____

_____

What other purpose would God have had in sending the spies to Jericho?

_____

_____

_____

One reason God sent the spies was to find Rahab and rescue her from destruction. He sent them for her salvation. And how much more did He do for us? **What a redeeming God we have! He will spare no expense and go to any lengths to bring about our salvation—including sending His Son, Jesus Christ, to this earth.**

In what other ways do you see the gospel pictured through Rahab's story?

_____

_____

_____

_____

_____

_____

_____

Write out a version of the gospel story in your own life. What was your identity before you came to know Jesus? What is it now? What lengths did God go to save you? If you're not yet a follower of Christ, write about how you'd like to see your identity changed.

_____

_____

_____

_____

_____

_____

_____

_____

_____

_____

Another Woman Who Needed Rescue

Joshua 2 isn't the only time we see God going out of His way to rescue and redeem.

John 4 records the story of Jesus' interaction with a Samaritan woman. Just as God providentially sent the Hebrew spies to seek out Rahab, Jesus Himself went out of His way to Samaria where He encountered the woman at the well.

- Like Rahab, this woman had a lifestyle of sexual sin.
- Like Rahab, she wasn't a part of the Israelites but was instead a citizen of Samaria.
- Like Rahab, she had heard stories about God and His people.
- And like Rahab, the Samaritan woman chose to put her faith in the one true God.

Read the whole account in John 4:1–45 and consider any other similarities between Rahab's story, the Samaritan woman's story, and your own story.

Day 3: *An Example of Faith*

Read Hebrews 11.

Hebrews 11 is often called the "Hall of Faith" because it's a list of many men and women who demonstrated deep faith in God. Of those mentioned, there are only two women named.

How are Rahab and Sarah similar? How are they different? Write your answers in the table below. (For context about Sarah, see Genesis 16; 18:1–21; 21:1–21.)

	SIMILARITIES	DIFFERENCES
Rahab		
Sarah		

Despite all of their differences, both of these women were redeemed out of their lost condition by the grace of God. And both of them are examples of faith.

Read Hebrews 11:30–31 below. Circle any words or phrases that stick out to you.

> By faith the walls of Jericho fell down after they had been encircled for seven days. By faith Rahab the prostitute did not perish with those who were disobedient, because she had given a friendly welcome to the spies.

According to verse 31, what outcome did Rahab deserve?

_____

_____

Find one other translation or paraphrase of Hebrews 11:31, and write it out below.

_____

_____

_____

Rahab was saved by faith. Her willingness to express hospitality to the spies was an evidence and expression of her faith.

How do you see God's amazing grace in the phrase "Rahab the prostitute did not perish"?

_____

_____

_____

At the beginning of Hebrews 11, the writer gives a description of faith. Write out that definition in your own words.

_____

_____

_____

_____

How did Rahab's actions show "assurance of things hoped for"?

_____

_____

_____

_____

What are you hoping for in your life today?

_____

_____

_____

_____

How can you choose to exercise faith in God as you wait?

_____

_____

Day 4: *Faith in Action*

Read James 2:14–26.

In James 2, the author makes a point about what kind of faith is saving faith … and holds up Rahab as an example.

Look at James 2:14–17 below. Underline any words or phrases that describe what true faith looks like, and circle and words or phrases that describe what it does *not* look like.

> What good is it, my brothers, if someone says he has faith but does not have works? Can that faith save him? If a brother or sister is poorly clothed and lacking in daily food, and one of you says to them, "Go in peace, be warmed and filled," without giving them the things needed for the body, what good is that? So also faith by itself, if it does not have works, is dead.

How does James describe faith apart from works (v. 17)?

_____

_____

_____

What does the Bible tell us about the importance of demonstrating our faith with actions? Look up the following passages and write your answer beside each one.

LUKE 10:25-37

JAMES 1:22-25

1 JOHN 3:17-18

According to pastor and Bible teacher Warren Wiersbe, "True saving faith can never be by itself: It always brings life, and life produces good works."[1] **If you have been truly saved, then your faith will be demonstrated in your behavior.**

In Hebrews 11, we find Rahab the prostitute linked with Sarah. James uses her and Abraham, the father of the Jewish faith, as illustrations of people who had dynamic, saving faith.

Read James 2:21–25.

List how this passage describes each person's faith.

ABRAHAM:

RAHAB:

James specifies that both Abraham and Rahab were justified by works. Look up the definition of *justification* in a Bible dictionary and write it below.

_____

_____

_____

_____

_____

_____

The theological definition of justification is "a declaration of righteousness." That means that **God sees us the same way that He sees His sinless Son.**

God's Word is clear that faith and grace are "the gift of God, not a result of works, so that no one may boast" (Eph. 2:8–9). We're not saved by what we do. We are saved by the grace of God expressed and exercised in our faith. However, the works of Abraham and Rahab demonstrated that they had in fact been made right with God and had saving faith.

In order for someone's faith to be true faith, it has to be backed up by some kind of action. We might believe intellectually that it's perfectly safe to jump out of an airplane. But if we're flying at 13,000 feet with a parachute strapped on our backs and refuse to jump, then we don't really believe it.

Think of someone whom you greatly admire for their faith in Christ. How do you see their faith put into action?

_____

_____

_____

_____

_____

_____

_____

How is your own faith evidenced by your works or actions?

_____

_____

_____

_____

_____

_____

_____

Rahab's faith led to a transformed life. **Genuine, saving faith always will.**

Is there evidence that . . .

- Your heart is being transformed?
- You're a new person?
- You've got a changed identity?
- You have new appetites and desires?
- You're headed in a new direction?

How did you answer the questions above? If you feel discouraged at what you see, turn to God and ask for help. He can transform your life for His glory.

Day 5: *Never Forget*

Read Psalm 107:1–2.

As we read the New Testament references to Rahab, there's another descriptor by her name. Look up Hebrews 11:31 and James 2:25 and write that word below.

_____

_____

_____

_____

If Rahab had a changed identity, why is she still referred to as "Rahab the prostitute"?

_____

_____

_____

_____

The Bible doesn't tell us specifics, but perhaps Rahab wanted to remember where God found her and what He had redeemed her from.

How can you remind yourself on a regular basis what God has rescued and redeemed you from?

_____

_____

_____

_____

Beyond that, Rahab's past was part of her life message. It was her God story, a means of reaching others with the grace of God.

If in the New Testament it just said "Rahab," we might forget. Rahab who? And we'd think, *Well, she must have been a great woman who deserved the grace of God.*

However, Scripture is not going to let us forget where she had been. Through her story, "Rahab the prostitute" is still sharing a message about God's grace and mercy.

With this in mind, what words do you now think of when you read the name "Rahab the prostitute"? Circle any below.

delivered

hope   redeemed

forgiven **grace**

made new

ASHAMED *sinful*

How can God use our past to reach others with His grace?

_____

_____

_____

Why are people drawn to others who openly share how God has delivered them from a sinful lifestyle?

_____

_____

_____

Often people will open up their hearts to someone who's transparent about the past and tell them things they'd never tell someone else—*because they know that person understands.* They know that person has been there. **They see in her not just where she's been but where God has brought her and how God has transformed her. And when they see her, they have hope.**

How does the story of Rahab the prostitute give you hope?

_____

_____

_____

_____

God also wants to use your story, no matter how messy it might be. It doesn't mean you have to name it everywhere you go. But **God wants to use your past—and His glorious grace in your life in overcoming it—as a message of grace and hope to share with others.**

Read Psalm 107:1–2 below. Underline what we, the redeemed of the Lord, are to do.

> Oh give thanks to the LORD, for he is good,
>   for his steadfast love endures forever!
> Let the redeemed of the LORD say so,
>   whom he has redeemed from trouble.

The NIV version of this passage says, "Let the redeemed of the Lord tell their story."

Why are we supposed to "say so," or share the stories of what God has done?

_____

_____

_____

_____

The ultimate purpose of the stories God has written in our lives is to give Him glory and point others back to Him. As we tell people how God has rescued and redeemed us, it's not just our story; it's the gospel story.

Your Story in Two Minutes

Like Rahab's story of redemption, your life story is a shining display of the gospel. Use this outline to write a version of your salvation story that can be shared in two to three minutes.

MY OLD LIFE

Describe your life before you came to believe in Jesus: your family and background as it relates to your faith journey, your need for Jesus (without sensationalizing past sin), etc.

HOW I CAME TO FAITH

Tell what drew you to Christ and how you became a Christian. In simple words, tell how through repentance and faith in the death and resurrection of Jesus, He is now your Lord. Focus on God as the author and hero of your story.

MY NEW LIFE

Tell how your old life and new life are different—including your attitude, character, and perspective. Share the joy and hope you have in Christ.

Once you've written your testimony, practice until it becomes natural. Then pray for opportunities to share your story and spread the message of God's matchless grace.

As you reflect upon our study of Rahab's life, answer the questions below.

What does Rahab's story teach me about the heart, the ways, and the character of God?

_____

_____

_____

_____

_____

How does her story point me to Jesus and the gospel?

_____

_____

_____

_____

_____

In the story of Rahab, is there an example to follow or avoid? If so, how should I seek to change in response?

_____

_____

_____

_____

_____

_____

_____

Ultimately Rahab's story points us to Jesus. She was far from God and enslaved to sin—like all of us! Then God rescued her from sin and redeemed her life.

As we've gone through this study, some of you may have felt like you were hearing your own story. It may be that you've had a background similar to Rahab or you've been in bondage to another sinful behavior or addiction. Or you may be on the opposite end of the spectrum. Maybe you've always tried to do what's right, to live a "good" life, and please the Lord. However, no matter what our behavior or our past, we need the grace of God as much as Rahab. Just like her, we are all candidates for His grace and unable to save ourselves. And just like her, God will rescue and redeem our lives. He'll give us a new identity and hope for the future.

Let's end our study not by focusing on who we once were, but who we are now as followers of Christ. Take time to reflect on 1 Peter 2:9–10 below and ask God to give you a fresh sense of His amazing grace.

> You are a chosen race, a royal priesthood, a holy nation, a people for his own possession, that you may proclaim the excellencies of him who called you out of darkness into his marvelous light. Once you were not a people, but now you are God's people; once you had not received mercy, but now you have received mercy.

Red Thread
VERSE

Rahab has a new identity; isn't that amazing? If you're a believer in Jesus, you do, too! You have a new family, a new status, and a new destiny. You have been redeemed! God looks at you and sees you as completely righteous in Jesus! Even though you still struggle with sin, there is a promise that you *will* be made completely clean and new. Now peek at where the Red Thread has led us—to ultimate happiness and no more sin and joyful worship and a place in God's kingdom!

> To him who loves us and has freed us from our sins by his blood and made us a kingdom, priests to his God and Father, to him be glory and dominion forever and ever. Amen. Behold, he is coming with the clouds, and every eye will see him, even those who pierced him, and all tribes of the earth will wail on account of him. Even so. Amen. (REV. 1:5-7)

Aren't you glad? Jesus is coming back! We are part of His great redemption story—and though this is the end of the study, we're still in the middle of the story. He's placed us into His family and community, the Church, and we get to walk along the scarlet thread on and on into eternity. He will come, and everyone will worship. He will make all things right and new. The scarlet thread will be revealed as the fabric of everything. We and everything that has been affected by sin will be redeemed. He will get glory. *Come soon, Lord Jesus!*

SMALL GROUP
DISCUSSION QUESTIONS

Week 1:

- What does Rahab's story reveal about God's character?
- Think of a time when God called you to do something that was bigger than you could handle on your own. How did you respond? How did God make you strong and courageous?
- What evidence of God's Providence (His care and guidance of all things) did you discover in Joshua 2?
- Through this first week of study, how did God use the life of Rahab to speak to you?

Week 2:

- How have you seen God at work in unlikely—or even corrupt—places?
- What are some examples from history when Christians might have felt it was necessary to lie? Do you think it's ever okay for a Christian to lie? Why or why not?
- Both Rahab and the Canaanites displayed fear of the Lord, albeit in different ways. As Christ-followers, how should we display a right fear of the Lord in our words and actions?
- What stories can we share about God working in our lives that could have an impact on those around us?
- Pray together with your group for opportunities to share Christ during the rest of this study.

Week 3:

- In what ways is God calling us to go against our world's culture today? What risks are we taking when we do? What rewards are available when we obey?
- Think of a time when you were confronted with the holiness and sovereignty of God. How did that change your view of Him?

 Listen in as women discuss this study in the Women of the Bible podcast by *Revive Our Hearts*. Find it at ReviveOurHearts.com/Rahab.

- What, if anything, did you have to leave behind when you chose to follow Christ? What have you gained since you came to faith in Him?

- How has God expressed His *hesed*, or lovingkindness, toward you? How have you shown it to others in your family? Your church? Your workplace? Your community?

- Take time to cry out to the Lord with your group for the salvation of people you care about who don't know Jesus as their Savior.

Week 4:

- In what areas of your life is obeying the Lord a challenge for you?

- Think about a time when your obedience to the Lord was visible for others to see. What effect did that have on your family? Members of your church? Non-believers around you?

- Why do we often feel like we have to have our lives in order before God can help us? How does Rahab's example help to free us from that way of thinking?

- How does knowing that though our "sins are like scarlet," God will make them "white as snow" (Isa. 1:18) help you move forward from your past?

- How can we take refuge in the blood of Jesus, just as Rahab took refuge in her home behind the scarlet cord?

Week 5:

- Think of a time when you've had to wait on the Lord—for Him to act, for an answer to prayer, for a resolution to a conflict, etc. What helped you the most to wait patiently for Him?

- What does a life ready for the return of Jesus look like? What do you need to change, if anything, for your life to be that way?

Listen in as women discuss this study in the Women of the Bible podcast by *Revive Our Hearts*. Find it at ReviveOurHearts.com/Rahab.

- What types of things tempt you to doubt God? What can you do to replace those doubts with the Truth of His promises?
- Share some of God's promises that you go to when you are struggling or going through a hard time. What is it about these promises that give you hope?
- How has Jesus been your refuge in the past? As you think about any current struggles you're facing, are you taking refuge in Him … or in something else?

Week 6:

- Share a bit about your own family history. How has God shown Himself to be faithful through your genealogy?
- How has your identity changed since you received Christ as your Savior—both spiritually and in other ways?
- What did you learn from Rahab's faith in action that you can apply to your own life?
- As you've studied Rahab's life, how have you grown in your understanding and appreciation of God's redeeming work in your life?
- What three main takeaways do you have from this study of Rahab?

Notes

Week 1: Written into God's Script

1 "H553 - 'Amats - Strong's Hebrew Lexicon (KJV)," Blue Letter Bible, accessed September 25, 2019, https://www.blueletterbible.org/lang/lexicon/lexicon.cfm?Strongs=H553&t=KJV.

2 Matthew George Easton, "Jericho," *Easton's Bible Dictionary* (Thomas Nelson, 1897), accessed June 6, 2019, https://www.studylight.org/dictionaries/ebd/j/jericho.html.

3 "First Fruits," That the World May Know, Focus on the Family, accessed June 6, 2019, https://www.thattheworldmayknow.com/first-fruits-article.

4 Ibid.

5 "2181. zanah," Strong's Concordance, accessed September 25, 2019, https://biblehub.com/hebrew/2181.htm.

6 "4204. porné," Strong's Concordance, accessed September 25, 2019, https://biblehub.com/greek/4204.htm.

7 "3830. pandocheus," Strong's Concordance, accessed September 25, 2019, https://biblehub.com/str/greek/3830.htm.

8 LeRoy E. Froom, "'Harlot' and 'Innkeeper,'" *The Ministry*, vol. 4, no. 9 (1931), https://www.ministrymagazine.org/archive/1931/09/harlot-and-innkeeper.

Week 2: The Mystery of God at Work

1 John Piper, "Is It Ever Right to Lie?", Desiring God, accessed July 8, 2019, https://www.desiringgod.org/interviews/is-it-ever-right-to-lie.

2 Jeff A. Benner, "What is the difference between lord, Lord, and LORD?" Ancient Hebrew Research Center, accessed October 12, 2019, https://www.ancient-hebrew.org/god-yhwh/difference-between-lord-Lord-and-LORD.htm.

3 Trent C. Butler, ed., *Holman Bible Dictionary* (Nashville: Holman, 1991), 497.

[4] Merrill F. Unger, *The New Unger's Bible Dictionary* (Chicago: Moody Bible Institute, 1988), 778.

[5] Butler, 497.

[6] "kēryssō," Blue Letter Bible, accessed August 16, 2019, https://www.blueletterbible.org/lang/lexicon/lexicon.cfm?Strongs=G2784&t=ESV.

[7] "Sharing Faith Is Increasingly Optional to Christians," Barna Group, 2018, https://www.barna.com/research/sharing-faith-increasingly-optional-christians/.

Week 3: The Lovingkindness of God

[1] "hesed," Blue Letter Bible, accessed July 31, 2019, https://www.blueletterbible.org/lang/lexicon/lexicon.cfm?page=5&strongs=H2617&t=ESV#lexResults.

[2] Iain Duguid, "Loyal-Love (Hesed)," Ligonier Ministries, November 1, 2011, https://www.ligonier.org/learn/articles/loyal-love-hesed/.

[3] Matthew Henry, "Joshua 2," *Matthew Henry's Complete Commentary on the Whole Bible*, https://www.studylight.org/commentaries/mhm/joshua-2.html.

[4] "hesed," Blue Letter Bible.

[5] Ibid.

[6] Will Kynes, "God's Grace in the Old Testament: Considering the *Hesed* of the Lord," *Knowing & Doing*, C.S. Lewis Institute, 2010, http://www.cslewisinstitute.org/webfm_send/430.

[7] Duguid.

[8] "hesed," Blue Letter Bible.

[9] Ibid.

[10] Charles Spurgeon, "Rahab's Faith," March 1, 1857, The Spurgeon Center, accessed July 30, 2019, https://www.spurgeon.org/resource-library/sermons/rahabs-faith#flipbook/.

Week 4: The Scarlet Cord

[1] "Discover the Bayeux Tapestry," Bayeux Museum, accessed September 6, 2019, https://www.bayeuxmuseum.com/en/the-bayeux-tapestry/discover-the-bayeux-tapestry/.

[2] M.G. Easton, "Colour," *Illustrated Bible Dictionary* (Thomas Nelson, 1897), 154.

[3] Nancy DeMoss Wolgemuth, "Choosing Joy over Fear," March 19, 2012, in *Revive Our Hearts*, podcast, https://www.reviveourhearts.com/podcast/revive-our-hearts/choosing-joy-over-fear/.

Week 5: The Big Picture

[1] "A Sunday Afternoon on the Island of La Grande Jatte," Artble.com, accessed September 10, 2019, https://www.artble.com/artists/georges_seurat/paintings/a_sunday_afternoon_on_the_island_of_la_grande_jatte.

[2] Anonymous, "My Life Is but a Weaving," Timeless Truths Free Online Library, Timeless Truths Publications, accessed September 10, 2019, https://library.timelesstruths.org/music/My_Life_Is_but_a_Weaving/.

[3] Ernst Sellin and Carl Watzinger, *Jericho die Ergebnisse der Ausgrabungen* (Osnabrück, Germany: Otto Zeller, 1973), 58. Quoted in Bryant Wood, "The Walls of Jericho," Answers in Genesis, March 1, 1999, https://answersingenesis.org/archaeology/the-walls-of-jericho/#fn_4.

[4] Ibid.

[5] Ibid.

Week 6: A New Identity

[1] Warren W. Wiersbe, *Be Mature: Growing Up in Christ* (Colorado Springs, CO: David C. Cook, 2008), 85.

Reflections

Reflections

MORE FROM

Revive Our Hearts™

RADIO • EVENTS • BLOGS

LEADERS

REVIVE OUR HEARTS . COM

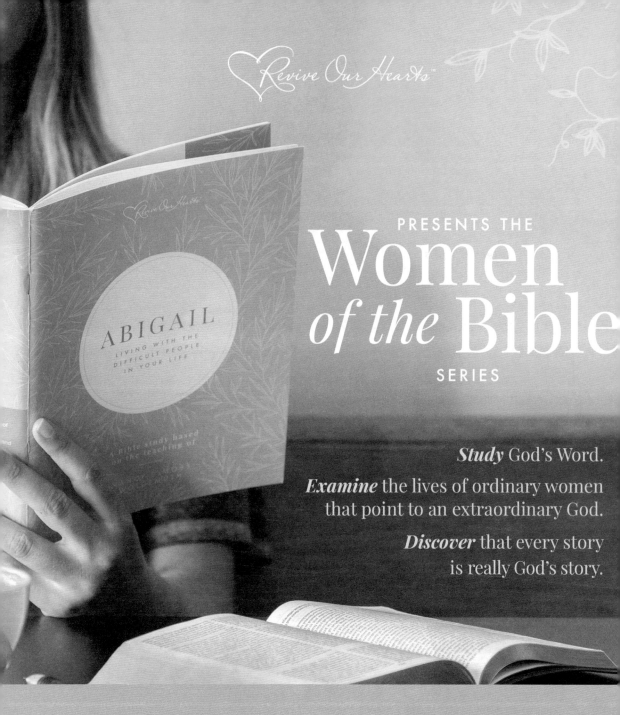